S.O.L.D.

THE **BREAKTHROUGH** **SYSTEM** TO SELL LESS AND MAKE MORE

EMERSON BRANTLEY
and TIMOTHY R. JOHNSON

S.O.L.D.

Designed and Published by
Celebrity Publishing
Las Vegas, Nevada, U.S.A
+1 702 997 2229
Sydney, Australia +61 2 8005 4878
CelebrityPublishers.com

For general information on our other products and services, please find our contact information online at www.Why2Wealth.com

To purchase customized or bulk copies of this book, please visit us online at www.CelebrityPublishers.com/bulk-books

ISBN: 978-1-922093-54-7

Thank you for investing in

S.O.L.D.

The Breakthrough System to Sell Less and Make More

Please visit the following websites for these bonus resources that will assist with the implementation of the concepts in this book:

Why-To-Wealth Blueprint™
www.MoreThanStrategy.com

Why-To-Wealth Action Questions™
www.Why2Wealth.com

About The Authors

ABOUT EMERSON BRANTLEY
(aka The Marketing Pirate, Captain Copy)

Founder of WEB3Direct.com, the Whytology™ Process Formula, Co-Founder of the Why-To-Wealth™ Marketing+Sales Strategy System (WhyToWealth.com)

As a Master Marketing Thought Leader, Strategist & High-Conversion Copywriter, Emerson Brantley has masterminded over 8,600 successful marketing campaigns, launches and tests for clients in the U.S. and 21 other countries. He is perhaps best known as creator of the longest-running lead-generating television infomercial ever aired — the "Cash Flow Generator" — generating millions in sales nationwide and 1500% growth, two Inc. 500 listings and a €132,000,000 IPO. His elegant marketing strategies and compelling copywriting has earned his reputation of creating often overwhelming results for his clients, such as 17,859 webinar registrations, 5,442 attendees for a single event, $10.52 EPC (Earnings Per Click) and $2.41 per email, 39% squeeze page opt-ins, 68.5% converted to offer (from cold Facebook leads) and 3000 media events in a single weekend. Direct Marketing guru Ted Nicholas called Emerson "One of the Country's Top 50 Marketing Copywriters, based on the ability to generate sales" like these.

His *Whytology*™ concepts have been relied on by speakers and thought leaders including John Assaraf, Dustin Mathews of Speaking Empire, real estate guru Ron LeGrand, National Trust expert Edwin Kelly, Dave Seymour of Flipping Boston and many others.

> "Emerson created the copy, the strategy and tweaked it to the point that our servers have been crashing on some of our campaigns!"
>
> — JOHN ASSARAF, NEUROGYM.

Emerson has been called upon by hundreds of companies and organizations as diverse as Fortune 100 giant Fruehauf, global airfreight leader Emery Worldwide, global corporate culture leader Partners In Leadership, Forbes School of Business, America's oldest non-profit American Forests, and Ministers of Tourism across the Caribbean. He has masterminded national joint ventures with Walmart, Walt Disney Epcot Center, Veterans of Foreign Wars, National Baseball Hall of Fame, Wright Brothers National Memorial at Kitty Hawk,

Jay Conrad Levinson,
Founder of Guerrilla Marketing, being honored for his Lifetime Achievement alongside Emerson Brantley, awarded Marketer of the Year.

and dozens more. Actual case histories and campaign results can be found at **www.WEB3Direct.com**

Combining his extensive marketing strategy and copywriting experience, Emerson has teamed up with business systemization and sales expert Tim Johnson to create the **Why-To-Wealth™ Marketing+Sales Strategy System.** Where Emerson's proprietary *Whytology*™ **Process** zeroes in and uniquely qualifies the most lucrative prospects in your market, Tim's **Proven S.O.L.D.™ Business Development Process** takes them by the hand, automating your entire customer acquisition and development process, increasing average and lifetime sales and allowing you to scale your business for unparalleled growth.

Emerson can be reached at:

Emerson@Why2Wealth.com
+1 904.419.7342

ABOUT TIMOTHY R. JOHNSON
(aka The King of Connections)

Founder of the S.O.L.D.™ Business Development Process,
Co-Founder of the Why-To-Wealth™ Marketing+Sales
Strategy System (WhyToWealth.com)

Recommended frequently by his network as the "Biz Dev Guy", Tim Johnson understands what it costs your business when your marketing and sales processes aren't smooth and consistent with every customer contact. Tim learned the hard way, by building several successful businesses, including as a general contractor and investor.

When he found his own success ended up consuming more and more of his life, Tim searched for solutions to streamline his operations, to fix the "holes" in his staffing, sales and marketing processes, and put in automated systems and processes that made sure his clients had the same experience, consistently, time and time again. His efforts paid off: Tim saw his business grow by double digits while cutting his workload by two-thirds.

He realized there were many others who were a **Smart, Talented, Unique, Person In Demand™ (S.T.U.P.I.D.™)** — experts in their space whose companies had the quality solutions their market craved. However, they either weren't getting the right message through to their Ideal Prospects or didn't have proven prospect-to-client systems to consistently retain more customers and boost the lifetime value of each one.

Combining his extensive experience systemizing business and sales solutions, Tim has teamed up with top marketing strategist and seasoned copywriter Emerson Brantley to create the **Why-To-Wealth™ Marketing+Sales Strategy System**. Where Emerson's proprietary **_Whytology™_ Process** zeroes in and uniquely qualifies the most lucrative prospects in your market, Tim's Proven **S.O.L.D.™ Business Development Process** takes them by the hand, automating your entire customer acquisition and development process, increasing average and lifetime sales and allowing you to scale your business for unparalleled growth.

Tim can be reached at:

Tim@Why2Wealth.com
+1 904.242.6738

To find out if your business qualifies for a "Boardroom" day to help you and your team get laser-focused on the mission-critical elements that will make — or break — your business, contact us using one of the options above.

In most cases, we will be able to eliminate the time and money-wasters that are holding you back, map out an easily-implemented Marketing and Sales Strategy, provide the copywriting for the exact Message To Market Match you need to reach your Ideal Prospects and get more of them to respond. We can help you systemize your entire process and, in the end, help you create the business you always wanted — one that provides for you, your family and employees, produces ongoing lead flow of qualified prospects, long-term value, Ideal Clients and the lifestyle you deserve. Contact us personally and we will quickly determine — usually in under ten minutes — if you qualify and how exactly we may be able to bring these advantages to your business.

In Praise of S.O.L.D.

"I have had the honor and privilege of knowing and working with both Tim and Emerson for several years, and I must say, they are two of the most cutting edge sales and marketing strategists I have ever come across.

I was delighted to know that these two brilliant minds have now teamed up to compile some of the best wisdom out there to help small businesses be successful in the marketplace.

There are many sales and marketing books, but this is more than just a book. This is a user's manual, a how-to guide to transform your business and more.

When you sit down to read this book, make sure you have a pen and a notepad nearby. Prepare to change your thinking, and your results.

Create immediately implementable business improvement strategies while you read this book...and your results will be nothing short of amazing.

This is a must read book for every Entrepreneur!"

— Jeannie Levinson, Co-Founder; CEO, Guerrilla Marketing International, www.gmarketing.com

"Emerson and Timothy have produced a book full of golden sales and marketing nuggets... from understanding who your customer is and what makes the tick, to how to best extract value from the relationships you nurture with your customers — make sure you have pen and paper to hand as you will have a myriad of ideas as you read through the book on ways you can improve your own businesses sales and marketing strategy."

— Barry Allaway, The Business Alchemist at Sales Funnels Made Simple, London — United Kingdom

"This book addresses an age-old problem in a fresh way — finally demystifying how Sales and Marketing can work together as a well-oiled machine...instead of at odds with each other. The authors tell it how it is, after decades of experience turning failing campaigns and companies into success stories. I recommend you implement these strategies before your competitors do!"

— Cydney O'Sullivan, CEO Millionaires Academy, Best Selling Author, Speaker and Business Strategist

"I've always had to struggle with referrals. I've never had a systemized process. One thing I love about Emerson is his "Pay It Forward" concept... they're presold, they don't care about price. Emerson has been amazing at helping me with that portion of my practice."

— Charlie Price, Attorney

"Copies of your presentation will be sent to every dealership in the Southeast as training material for their sales staff. Congratulations, Emerson, on a job well done!"

— **John E. Pierson, District Sales Manager, Southeast Toyota Distributors, LLC, World's largest franchised Toyota Distributorship with 166 dealers.**

"I'd be surprised if there are more than 50 copywriters in the entire U.S. who can meet the only real-world test with meaning — the ability to create sales. One of them is Emerson Brantley. He is an excellent communicator in all media, including print, TV and the Internet."

— **Ted Nicholas, International Direct Marketing Consultant, "Grandfather" of Direct Mail Marketing**

"Emerson has thirty years of experience but more than that he has thirty years of results. If you're like me — you're really good at what you do but not that good at marketing — He'll ask you the questions and you'll be able to come up with the answers that will enable you to position yourself and take your business to the next level."

— **Shirley Dalton, Australia's Business Systemizer**

"I was in corporate America for nearly 20 years. His wisdom, guidance and direction have made a huge impact in my business. He is a Master."

— **Vicki Higgins, CEO Accelerated Shift Marketing**

"I didn't want to launch a product, I wanted to launch a corporation. The branding, the relationships you maintain... Emerson was able to give me strong perspective on just how to implement all that. It is such a pleasure to work with someone who looks at not just how to accomplish tasks, but how to accomplish dreams."

— Jennifer Puterbaugh, Propel Point

"Emerson Brantley has helped us articulate exactly what our message is. Each step he's helped us reach out to millions of people around the world with a message of hope and inspiration. I highly, highly recommend his services to anybody that would need somebody to truly make a difference in their organization."

— Mark Kaplan, Venture Capitalist,
   Founder Club Asteria Foundation

"I learned things I didn't know in 25 years of running a successful business. One takeaway was that marketing is not 'a marketing campaign,' marketing never, ever ends and that's something I'm going to do."

— Alison Palmer, Past National President, ARCSI
   (Association of Residential Cleaning Services International)

"My time with Emerson has been awesome. He's been able to get inside my head and pull out of me my vision that I want for my company, and I really haven't met anybody that's been able to do that... to guide and

focus my business to the next level and the next level beyond that. It took Emerson to pull it out of me."

— **Pat Gage, Speaker, Author, Developer**

"Emerson Brantley gave me one of the most important insights that any marketer ever has, that one of the most important things I can do is offend the 97% of the people that are not my market. That is just revolutionary, because the amount of resources that I would be losing ... could be millions of dollars. I just want to thank Emerson for his amazing insights and his great marketing skills."

— **J.V. Crum, ConsciousMillionaire.com, former owner trucking corporation**

"During our initial meeting, he understood the business I was in and had some immediate suggestions on how to increase my business in my email by that afternoon. He has since suggested several avenues on how to reduce my cost of reaching my market. Not only is Emerson an excellent writer, he understands business."

— **John Hayes, Jr., CEO TCI Publishing**

"Emerson understands every business model and every sales and marketing funnel; He's got versatility across the scope of many industries so he's very flexible, very versatile, extremely professional."

— **Angela Albright, CEO Automate My Online Marketing**

"Emerson has the perfect mix of marketing expertise and flexibility. He listened closely to my ideas and molded them into a spectacular idea that has nationwide appeal. He provided what most advertising consultants could not, a very keen sense of your business goals and how to formulate them into something meaningful and actionable."

— **Dean Rice, <u>BikeTrip.com</u>, The "Million Mile Challenge"**

"If you have the chance to work with this gentleman he understands the psychology of what it takes to really relate to somebody, grab their attention...explain your business in words way better than your own and in the end actually have them purchase what you are selling!"

— **Adam Urbanski, Millionaire Marketing Mentor**

Acknowledgements

No endeavor can ever be truly a one-person project. We all depend on others to help make our vision a reality, and this book is no different. A special thanks to my amazing wife, former professor and artist Anne Banas, who has endured countless hours when I've been "in the zone" writing and creating marketing programs and projects, or traveling to speak in distant cities or work with some client onsite. Writing this book has been no different. Thank you Anne for loving and supporting me so good through it all lo these 20 years (I'm looking forward to the next 20 with you too!)

Those who know me know I give a lot of credit for my successes to the influence of all the powerful women in my life, starting with my mom, who I feel I know better now than when she and my dad passed away in 1983. I've been blessed with two incredible older sisters and the greatest mother-in-laws imaginable. Three daughters, four granddaughters (and yes, one grandson)...I think you see the trend. Thank you for the powerful feminine energy and intuitive insights that have helped me understand that speaking to our clients' inner Whys is much more important than a lot of fancy product knowledge and hype. People really don't care how much you know until they know how much you care.

Thank you George and Katie Wood, for your amazing album that ended up in my home as a kid. Your ability to weave words is a major part of how I think about writing even today.

Unlike so many in marketing, I spent ten years in face-to-face selling. I was fortunate that my first real sales job, with Emery Worldwide, provided me training through IBM's landmark Personal Selling Skills...all based on building mutually-beneficial relationships and listening to your prospects. Years later I realized that I approached every aspect of marketing and sales this way, and the principles of Whytology show how important this customer first mindset is.

This attitude is what really brought me and Tim Johnson together in the first place. As Tim says, I write and market like he sells, with the intention of bringing real solutions that add value to our Ideal Prospects and Clients...not to just close a sale. So here's a a special thanks to my partner on this project and Why To Wealth, Tim Johnson.

I've had the privilege of working with many business and marketing minds over the years, including greats like Gary Halbert and Ted Nicholas, one of the "godfathers" of direct marketing, who took me under his arm and personally mentored me. My early time at Combined Insurance under the guidance of W. Clement Stone ingrained a lifetime of positive outlook that always sees the hidden possibilities, and helps me see the opportunities in just about any business. Probably my greatest business influence was W. Edwards Deming. He changed Japan and he validated my approach to marketing: you can always improve your results, no matter how good. There are too many to thank here but I learned from each of you.

In writing, the devil's in the details, and I can't say enough about the editing and publishing team that made this final product what it is...a professionally-produced book that can hold its own among truly game changing books on business growth, marketing and sales.

Finally, with her calm presence just outside my office door and her deep insights that always lick sticky mental challenges, a thanks to our Abby, the Rottweiler who rescued us and joined our pack. Now we can make up some of the walks we've missed while pulling this book together!

Table of Contents

SECTION ONE
Strategy (Marketing+Sales)

CHAPTER 1

CHAPTER 2

CHAPTER 3

CHAPTER 4

CHAPTER 5

Introduction

The Breakthrough System to Sell Less and Make More —
Bridging the Marketing-Sales Divide to Create a Marketing
and Sales Continuous Improvement Loop

> "Remember, son, marketing is an expense…
> it's sales that brings in the money."

I was a new junior executive, charged with creating marketing programs for five divisions of a Fortune 100 corporation. The man laying down the law was none other than the president himself. His words made no more sense to me then than they do now.

Marketing and Sales are two sides of the same coin, with the same ultimate objectives. I was reminded of my place in the grand scheme of things regularly by other C-suite suits after that. Sadly, I don't ever recall a single time at any company where Marketing and Sales worked together, side-by-side, on a single campaign.

Chances are, your company has a similar disconnect between marketing and sales — maybe even some competition or resentments. It is so culturally ingrained, most owners and managers are blind to it, and in denial that it even exists within their organization. Even "solo-preneurs" aren't immune. After reading this book, I predict you will see where these issues are costing you untold amounts of money each year.

> "After reading this book, I predict you will see where these issues are costing you untold amounts of money each year."

In fact, this mindset can be costing you as much *or more* than your total current revenues — the money you collect — both in wasted resources and lost opportunities. Based on our work with thousands of entrepreneurs, business owners and corporate executives across the U.S. and in 21 other countries, the amount is almost always greater than the costs of bringing us or other experts in to fix the problem.

Even more important than lost revenue, this issue costs businesses time, energy and untold millions of dollars, throwing good money after bad, never knowing for sure if your message is anything more than "in the ballpark". As John Wanamaker, department store magnate (1838-1922) famously declared:

> ## "Half the money I spend on advertising is wasted — the trouble is, I don't know which half."

Perhaps worst of all, most marketing or sales presentations, training books and even consultants don't really shed much light on solving this, even though they offer many tactical "solutions" you may or may not need.

So, what makes this book any different?

Unlike other approaches, in this book we bring your sales and marketing together in a single, united **Marketing+Sales Strategy** that will *"bridge the gap"*. You will discover the exact steps to break down the walls and create a single focus, and how this will impact your results from both sides — Tim Johnson, from the sales perspective and me, Emerson Brantley, from the marketing side.

Who is this for?

Generally, this book is written for you if you have a marketing team (or person) *and* a sales team (or salesperson) and:

- Your marketing strategy isn't working like it did… if it ever did.
- Your sales and marketing teams aren't aligned or producing at the levels you know they can.
- Your marketing message isn't reaching the right people or getting the response you need.
- Your business is at a plateau or reaching for bigger growth than you're achieving.
- You aren't getting paid what you should be for the value you give your clients now.
- You find it increasingly difficult to distinguish yourself from your competitors.

☑ Your team wastes too much time on high-maintenance clients that generate smaller revenues, instead of focusing on high-revenue/low-maintenance ones.

Truth be told, this book applies to you even if you contract with outside sales or marketing providers, or your marketing and sales teams are one and the same. Even if the same person handles both — *even if* that person is you, and you alone.

Why should you believe or trust us?

If you've read through our professional bios at the beginning of this book, you will discover I've been a Master Strategist and Copywriter in over 8,600 campaigns in the U.S. and 21 other countries. My proprietary **Whytology™ Process Formula** is the result of having over $100 million during my career to test and prove what works, and what doesn't.

This has been true online — with results such as a $4.3 million product launch, $10.52 earnings per click and 64.5% conversions — as well as "old-school", creating 3,000 media events in a single weekend, or developing the longest-running profitable, lead-generating infomercial ever. Whether as a Wall Street Journal bestselling author, international speaker, mentor, consultant or coach for Fortune 100 companies, startups, entrepreneurs, small businesses, non-profits and even ministers of tourism, it's safe to say that, in marketing strategy and messaging, I've "been there, done that!"

You'll see that Tim Johnson is a serial entrepreneur and real estate investor, best-selling author, speaker, trainer and coach. Known by some as the "Biz Dev Guy", by others as the "Sales Whisperer," he guides and coaches onsite sales teams internationally and at dozens of events each year. He regularly breaks longstanding sales records using the approaches we share in this book, following his proprietary **S.O.L.D.™ Process**, which you'll learn about later in this book.

Tim and I realized that he approached sales and I approached marketing from the same methodology, and so we brought the two together and called it the **Why-To-Wealth Strategy System™**.

Individually and together, we have conducted in-depth Marketing+Sales Strategy "Boardroom" days for clients in the U.S. and internationally. These clients invest from $25,000 to $200,000, or more, to have us drill down and reveal the insights we are sharing in this book, or even more for us to help them implement these concepts in their businesses. It must be effective — we guarantee where others don't, and our clients realize vastly greater ROI (return on investment) than the investment itself. So, we encourage you to recognize the value of this to you and your company or organization, and put these concepts into practice for yourself.

> "…we encourage you to recognize the value of this to you and your company or organization, and put these concepts into practice for yourself."

Is this worth your time and effort — and your money? What will Your ROI be?

Ask yourself, how much difference will it make when your *marketing is done right*? Your selling process will be so much easier. You'll no longer need strong closers — order-takers will do just fine. And what will it mean when your *sales are done right*? They'll provide marketing with the missing tools they need, to get better at finding Ideal Clients (or customers, or patients, etc.) at lower costs, getting more of them to respond — and *buy*.

What will it mean for your business when:

- ☑ Your sales and marketing teams are working together in synch, producing the results you know they can?
- ☑ Your marketing message is reaching the right people with the right message, and they are responding in greater numbers?
- ☑ Your business requires less of your time, is less stressful, and produces greater revenues?
- ☑ You can focus *on* your business instead of working long hours *in* it?
- ☑ You finally have the time to enjoy the fruits of your labor and the lifestyle you deserve?

When this powerful Marketing+Sales Strategy is in place, an amazing transformation begins to happen in your business. By understanding what we call your Ideal Clients' "**Whytology™**" — their hidden drivers that compel them to do business with you, and *only* you — you will begin to experience dramatic improvements in your customer acquisition and sales processes that will:

- **REDUCE Your Sales Cycle**
- **IMPROVE Your Sales per Lead**
- **INCREASE Your Revenues Per Customer**
- **SIMPLIFY Your Sales Process**

In the next several chapters, you will discover how starting with the simple question "Why?" can lead you directly to that motherlode of Ideal Clients and create a literal "force field" around you, keeping the others away. This will allow you to put the famous "80/20 Rule" to work in your favor, *BEFORE* you waste another minute trying to "sell" to the wrong people. Using the power of "Why?" you will be able to focus ALL your time, efforts, energy and dollars on the 20% of your market who already wants you — they just don't know it yet!

How this book is structured

We've organized this book into two main sections, based on our proprietary **S.O.L.D.™ Business Development Process**:

- **Strategy (Marketing+Sales)**
- **Objections = Opportunities**
- **Leveraging Referrals**
- **Duplicate & Automate**

Strategy must come before Tactics, so we will spend the entire first half of the book walking through the key steps to create the perfect Marketing+Sales Strategy. We will cover the *Why, Who* and *What* that define your strategy and help guide you on every tactical decision you will ever need to make — the **Where, When** and *How* of your marketing. There are plenty of voices telling you which online or offline tactics to use. Get your Strategy right and the rest is easy.

> "We encourage you to not just read this book in a casual way, but assume the insights and concepts we have included can give you game-changing wisdom to take your business to the next level and beyond."

We will cover how to strategically use your message and methods to eliminate more of the people you don't want and attract more of the ones you do. You will discover how this engages the Pareto Principle — a.k.a. the 80/20 Rule — to work *FOR* you, instead of against you. In the process, you will get more, higher qualified leads for less cost, and they will covert much easier and buy more than you probably experience now.

In the second half, we will show how Objections=Opportunities, how — with the right 100,000-foot Strategy — your salespeople can literally become order-takers, and how this will increase your bottom line dramatically. You will see how important metrics are, and how building a **Marketing+Sales Partnership** will revolutionize your marketing with priceless "soft intel" data your Customer Relationship Management (CRM) program cannot provide.

It is common wisdom that inbound sales are easier than outbound, that repeat customers are worth more and buy more than new leads, and that referrals are much better than cold or even warm leads. Of these, the least understood and most under-utilized are referrals. In **Leveraging Referrals** we'll cover two kinds: Ideal Client referrals and partner referrals.

Finally, almost everything in your marketing can be systemized so leads, prospects and clients never fall through the cracks. In **Duplicate & Automate**, we'll show how we work with our clients to standardize and systemize your marketing, so your customers will feel the love — and keep coming back for more!

We encourage you to not just read this book in a casual way, but assume the insights and concepts we have included can give you game-changing wisdom to take your business to the next level and beyond. If it has the power to do that, it deserves your focused attention. And it does, but only with your active engagement. So, we suggest you:

1. Set aside uninterrupted time to read through each chapter and section.
2. Have a pen and pad ready to take physical notes. Putting pen to paper has been shown to help cement new concepts far greater than using a keyboarc or tablet.
3. Write more than notes or reminders. Write the thoughts they trigger, how they apply to you and your business, and the actions you need to take to put them into place sooner rather than later.
4. After reading through this book once, while taking notes, go through it again with your notes. You will be surprised at how going all the way through may have changed some of your earlier observations, and how much your original notes will have evolved in the process.

5. As you go through it, take decisive action on what you read. Don't wait until the end to begin to reevaluate your marketing and sales. There is no power in the printed words in this book, only in the actions you take to apply these time-tested, proven, real-world insights and concepts — this experiential wisdom — to work in your life, with your business, today.

Other resources

We've helped hundreds of clients in thousands of campaigns spanning 21 countries, so the insights here are from direct, first-hand experience in the real world. With some we've done in-depth consulting, others actual campaign development and sales management. We've distilled all our experience into this book as well as in some online resources that may be helpful as you develop your own Strategies and Tactics.

These two downloads will help clarify what we've covered in this section

Why-To-Wealth Blueprint
www.MoreThanStrategy.com

Why-To-Wealth Action Questions
www.Why2Wealth.com

We hope you take advantage of these insights and resources to guide you, so you can create this powerful **Marketing+Sales Strategic Partnership** in your company, and experience the amazing difference it will make to your bottom line. Are you ready? Let's get started!

Carpe diem!

EMERSON BRANTLEY
TIMOTHY R. JOHNSON

THE SECRET OF CHANGE IS TO FOCUS ALL YOUR ENERGY NOT ON FIGHTING THE OLD BUT ON BUILDING THE NEW

Socrates

Section One

STRATEGY
(Marketing+Sales)

"Strategy comes from knowing your Vision and Value. Your 'Why' gives you your vision. Their 'Why' gives you your Value. It all starts with 'Why'."

— EMERSON BRANTLEY, CO-FOUNDER OF THE WHY-TO-WEALTH STRATEGY SYSTEM™

CHAPTER 1

Strategy Before Tactics

> "Stop selling your dreams and sell them
> what they want — their own dreams."
>
> — TIM JOHNSON, CO-FOUNDER
> OF THE WHY-TO-WEALTH STRATEGY SYSTEM™

What's your Strategy? Where do you get business? Where do you start your marketing?

When we ask this question, we get answers that range from '*What*' companies sell, their products or services, and why they're superior to others, to the demographics they're looking for in a customer — their '*Who*', or '*Where*' they'll find them, like conferences or mailing lists.

In my experience, the focus is almost always on different tactics and techniques like, "Should I use Facebook ads or AdWords?" "Are solo ads or email better?" "What about Pinterest or Snapchat or

LinkedIn or podcasts — how do I monetize them?" "What about all the offline, old-school methods like direct mail, TV, radio and print — do they still work?" In sales, it's the same. "Let's try this new sales path." "You need a better closing script." "More prospecting."

Strategy comes before Tactics

Marketing events, companies and experts seem to offer no end of new programs, apps, software and other "shiny objects" or opinions about the best **Where, When and How** to market your products or services, and all your tactical decisions. The truth is, until you figure out the **right Marketing and Sales Strategy for you and your business**, you're sort of like Alice asking the Cheshire Cat for directions, with no sense of where she wanted go:

> "Well, that depends a good deal on where you want to get to," said the Cat.
> "I don't much care where—" said Alice.
> "Then it doesn't matter which way you go," said the Cat.
> "—So long as I get somewhere," Alice added as an explanation.
> "Oh, you're sure to do that," said the Cat, "if you only walk long enough."

This has often been used in goal-setting and motivational talks, but it's significantly greater than that. As we will see, goals result from your strategy, not the other way around. And if you don't have a **Crystal Clear Strategy**, any old tactic will probably work about as good as any other.

Strategy: Your "100,000-foot" Vision and the Value You Bring

Whether we call it the **Why-To-Wealth Strategy System™**, the **S.O.L.D.™ Process** or **Whytology™**, **you must be crystal-clear about who you don't want, and who you do** — that is, **your Ideal Client**. Taking the time to lock down your overall strategy first — *before* choosing your tactics — is the most important step you can take to achieve the successful and profitable marketing results you want. What if you could KNOW:

- ☑ The inner mind of your prospect and what they feel? You *CAN*.
- ☑ The reasons why they buy in such detail that you can speak directly to their drivers — the emotional, intuitive feelings that *compel* them to want to do business with you or not? You *WILL*.
- ☑ They already believe and trust that you — and you alone — are their very best option, even if they haven't found you yet? They *DO*.

It all starts with one question: "Why?"

Knowing your *WHY* and, even more importantly, the *WHYS* your Ideal Clients need answered before they decide *you, and you alone,* are who they want to do business with, is the key to having a powerful, successful Marketing Strategy. Most marketers skip this first, critical step completely, choosing who they think they want or what they think will sell, before knowing their *Why* first.

It may seem like determining who you want or don't want is straightforward, but you need to know your *Why* before you even figure out your *Who*. You need to know *Why* they're going to buy from you to help you understand *Who* they are in the first place. Once you get the *Why* dialed in...

Knowing their **Why determines** your **Who.** Knowing your **Who determines** your **What.**

These are the core to creating your Powerful Marketing Strategy

All your tactical options, the *Where*, *When* and *How* marketing decisions regarding your Message and Methods, become relatively easy once your Strategy is clear. After all, it doesn't matter what online or offline channels or methods you choose; if you don't know *Why* your prospects will buy from you — that is, why they *MUST buy from YOU* — you will never achieve the results or growth you want and need. In the next chapter, we will find out exactly why your Ideal Clients want you and what you market.

CHAPTER 2

Your Vision: Start with Why

"Never — absolutely never
compromise your principles."

— MARY KAY ASH

Your 100,000-foot Vision

Your Vision isn't about fancy statements written on your site and in your materials. It's about the core of *Why* you do what you do, including your higher purpose that guides you in business and in life. **People don't care how much you know until they know how much you care.**

Imagine you are a high-flying aircraft. Most jets can only fly to about 50,000 feet, and you get a pretty good view of cities and land at that height. But let's say you were flying at twice that, 100,000 feet, high enough to begin to see the curve of the earth and entire countries in your view. This vision gives you crystal-clear understanding of how it all fits together. The chaos and confusion on the ground would be far enough away that you could begin to see solutions to challenges you'd never seen before.

> "The only way we have found to cure these ills is to get everyone on the same page, understanding the overall strategy for your business."

It's like that with your Marketing Strategy. When most people think about their marketing, it immediately devolves into finding the right tactics — the right message, using the best methods — and that can quickly become confusing and overwhelming. Sales, for many, seems much more straightforward but, as we'll see later, there are plenty of sales plans that confuse and overwhelm sales teams. Plus, we've already mentioned that the two teams most often operate separately from each other, and not always on friendly terms.

The only way we have found to cure these ills is to get everyone on the same page, understanding the overall strategy for your business. When we do our intensive "Boardrooms" with clients, often we'll see team members answering each other's tactical questions with these words:

"Well, what's our Strategy?"

Try this yourself now, and especially later in the process. Go through your list of tactics that you are using, thinking about using or have been told is the best for you. Then examine each one in the same way, by asking this same question. Here are some examples of different tactics our clients ask us about regularly:

- "Should we use Facebook Live or YouTube?"
- "Is email marketing right for us?"
- "What about joint ventures, solo ads and list sharing?"
- "Would radio or TV help us reach our market better?"
- "Should we invest money in print, in magazines or papers?"
- "Does podcasting make sense for our market?"
- "What kind of message do we need to be sending?"
- "What would be the best offer or call to action to use?"

As we shared in the introduction, there are plenty of voices trying to convince you that this or that way is the best — so how do you know what's best for your company, product or service?

Well, what's your Strategy?

You see, every tactical approach will work for some company, for some product or service, for some market, for some price, at some time. The only way to make these tactical decisions is to have a **Crystal Clear Strategic Vision that can only come from answering, "Why?"**

There are two people whose Whys are important — You, and your Ideal Client

In any relationship, there must be value added from both sides. Otherwise, it's an unhealthy relationship that will struggle and probably eventually fail. Yet in business, we tend to only think of OURSELVES as adding the value, with our customers paying US for it. We flatten out who our Ideal Clients are and make that the sum of the relationship.

Clients are a lot more complex than that — and so are you, by the way. We all have inner drivers that influence our decisions and compel us to choose our options in certain ways. As marketers, once we get this, we can begin building long-term relationships of value. It all starts with asking, "Why?" Here's how it works.

Answer your "Why"

Start by getting clear about your own *Whys*, personally or as a company. This is important because it gives you your **Vision.**

- Why are you as good as you are?
- Why do you do what you do?
- Why do you get up and go to work every day?

Your Vision is what drives you to face the frustrations and challenges of running a business. It's where your purpose and passion come into play, and your dreams of the life and lifestyle you want for you, your family and your team.

It should also include your "higher purpose", something more important than your business or you. That charitable or social cause that you believe will make a difference in the world. This is something more than a round bin for customers to bring in canned goods and get a discount. This is a cause, a passion that you relate to and align with, that you are willing to identify yourself and your company with, and that you are committed to helping succeed. That's why understanding and recognizing your own *Why* is important — because it gives you your **Vision**.

> **Tim adds:** "Now, here's what's important to remember. At the end of the day, your market doesn't really care about your *Whys*, your needs or your dreams. They may very well relate to your higher purpose. If you have connected your marketing with a social purpose or non-profit, that may become a deciding factor for them. But, for the most part, what they care about most, what we *ALL* care about most is..."

WIIFM: What's In It For Me?

You've probably heard this before — you must answer their WIIFM to make the sale. How do you know the answers? By taking the time to understand their *Why!*

It doesn't stop with the marketing. Later, we'll talk about how your sales team needs to continue in this same mindset and sell to your customers' dreams, not yours.

IT'S NOT JUST ABOUT THE IDEAS IT'S ABOUT MAKING THE IDEAS HAPPEN

CHAPTER 3

Your Value – Answering Their Why

> "Strive not to be a person of success,
> but rather a person of VALUE."
>
> — ALBERT EINSTEIN

Knowing and answering your Ideal Clients' *Why* questions satisfactorily is even more important than your own, because *their* Why is what gives you *your* **Value — your Unique Value Proposition, or UVP**.

Your Value isn't about your dignity or worth as a human being. In business, your value is 100% about the ***Value You Bring to your Ideal Clients***. Therefore, it's so important to understand all the *Whys* your Ideal Clients need you to answer *BEFORE* they decide to pay attention to you and your message— and respond to it.

> "In business, your value is 100% about the 'Value' you can provide for your ideal clients."

Some of their *Whys* are deeply embedded, like looking smart, making the "right" decisions, being decisive, etc. Others are more circumstantial, like frustration or weariness from dealing with the problem or issue that you can solve. Marketers call these drivers "psychographics", and once you know them, they will help you understand your Ideal Clients better and encourage more to respond. Take the time to step inside their minds and ask the questions they're thinking about right now:

- Why will they listen to you? (They have lots of options)
- Why should they believe you can solve their problem, (issue, frustration or pain)?
- Why are you any different? (They've been over-promised and under-delivered before)
- Why should they trust you, or even care? (Is this important enough to take a chance?)
- Why do they need what you offer? (It takes a lot to change)
- Why should they buy from you? (Maybe they should shop around first)
- Why should they buy from you *NOW?* (What's the urgency that causes them to decide?)
- ...and all the other *Whys* you need to know to launch a successful campaign.

Can you feel the difference this makes? When you take the time to care enough to respect and answer your clients' inner drivers, you can expect them to respond with three magic words:

"Tell me more!"

No, it's not, "Where do I sign?" or, "How do I pay?" "Tell me more," means they are open to you, their defenses have dropped a bit, and they trust you a little more than before. Get enough *tell me mores* and you'll have a customer for life.

Think of it this way. You're on a blind date, and the conversation sounds like Charlie Brown's teacher. "Wah wah wah wah wah…" It's all one-way. No interest in you or your thoughts or feelings — it's all about them. No way you're going to lean over and say, "Really? Tell me more!" Before long, you're checking your phone and making excuses to leave.

Now, suppose you're on another date and the person is engaging, asking about your thoughts and ideas, sharing theirs. You're on the edge of your seat, interested, intrigued and encouraging them to *"tell me more."* This is the beginning of a potentially great relationship.

> **Tim adds:** "Tell me more" can begin with a response to an ad or click-through from an email. It can also be a phone call from your Sales team, or when a client opts in on your landing page for more information. It can be their first purchase or consultation, their next, the one after that and so on. The point is you can take all the pressure off yourself to 'make the sale' when you start seeing them for who they are and being genuinely interested

in doing what's best for them. The only buy-in you ever need is "tell me more." That's the beginning and continuation of a lifetime relationship of value.

Figuring out our customers' *Why* questions is the beginning, because we know what we're looking for in our *Who*. Now it's time to figure out just *Who* they really are.

CHAPTER 4

Determine Your "Who" – Your Ideal Client

> "Decide Who you DON'T want first, and you'll know exactly Who you DO want."
>
> — EMERSON BRANTLEY

Once you get clear about their *Whys*, you can begin defining exactly *Who* these people are. Can you see how this process goes way beyond "pain points" and "hot buttons", "overcoming objections" and "hammer closes"? It isn't about speaking to some imaginary avatar, but the living, breathing, emotional, complex person that your Ideal Client really is. Most marketers and salespeople identify their prospects by **demographic** information — their age, gender, ethnicity, marital status, income and all the other profile selections you've chosen. In business-to-business marketing, these may be types of business, number of employees, contact title, etc.

Other than a few, such as age, gender and ethnicity, **all demographics are the results of decisions people have made**. Even among the two or three 'fixed' selections, people are increasingly able to choose how they are seen. Age and especially ethnicity have long been iffy. As for gender, Facebook alone now has 71 gender options!

> "It isn't about speaking to some imaginary avatar, but the living, breathing, emotional, complex person that your Ideal Client really is."

So, if demographics are history, based on their past decisions, *Why* did they make the decisions they made? Why indeed! What inner drivers are ones you can speak directly to? Perhaps now you can see *WHY* is where we start first to better understand and select our *WHO*.

Tim adds: "Marketers call this *'psychographics'*, because demographics are just the things about them that are easy to see, like how old they are, the car they drive, their income, etc. But when you crawl inside their heads, you start to see through their eyes. Marketing does it by looking at their demographic decisions and asking *Why* they made them. Sales has an advantage here because they can ask those probing questions that get clients to open up and tell us more. 'How's that working in your life?' 'Did that get you what you wanted?' 'What happened that kept you from getting it?'"

Sales gathers all sorts of "soft intel" that Marketing can use, but most Sales organizations never share what they know with the Marketing team.

Whytology™ begins where all the demographics end. Using this methodology, you can reach down inside your Ideal Market and do a literal "mind-meld" so you can really *get them.* Sometimes, you'll understand them better than they do themselves — their fears, frustrations, stomach knots and deep-seated needs — and you can speak directly to those inner forces with the solutions they feel they need most.

Imagine being able to clearly separate the ones you want from the ones you don't. So, instead of wasting countless hours on people who are not your Ideal Clients, you can spend more quality time developing the Ideal Client relationships that matter, that work and are the most lucrative.

TIP: Avoid terms like "anyone", "everyone" and "whoever".

You Don't Want Everyone! There is NO company, product or service that will ever reach 100% of all possible buyers. There are over 7.3 billion people in the world. There are over 325 million in the U.S. alone. There is only one you, so decide — choose who you *DON'T* want <u>first</u>!

Stop and think about it — you don't want the whiners, complainers, nothing-is-good-enough, the tire-kickers or the deadbeats, right?

> *"The better you get at defining Who you don't want, the clearer you will become on exactly Who it is you do want."*

This exercise will almost immediately move you into the ideal psychographic characteristics of your market. The better you get at defining Who you don't want, the clearer you will become on exactly Who it is you *DO* want, and what your Ideal Clients need to hear to respond — and buy.

Now you can set about finding out who that person is demographically. Defining demographics is easy to figure out when you start by eliminating the people you don't want.

Who IS your Ideal Client?

I often describe my Ideal Client this way:

- They listen to you and follow your advice.
- They trust you.
- They buy from you again and again.
- They forgive you when you screw up (and we all do at some point!)
- They refer people to you (endlessly).

These are your raving fans, ambassadors, evangelists, etc. Who wouldn't want more of these, and less of the others? The more you refine your message to attract these people, the more your message resonates with their *Whys* and the more you will repel the ones you don't want!

It's like Yin and Yang - The Law of Attraction has an opposite but equally important Law of Repulsion.

Have you ever had a friend who went from one bad relationship to another? Sooner or later, someone must have a talk with them, tell them to "look in the mirror!." It's important for them to recognize that they are attracting the people they don't want! So stop it!

Yet in marketing and sales, people say things like, "All money's green!" and, "Get all you can, can all you get!" without regard to whether the fit is right or not. This leads to bad relationships and reviews, as well as damaged morale, dignity and self-esteem for your people. So, stop it!

You cannot be all things to all people. You don't even want to be. Try selling to everyone and you'll sell to no one!

Start sending out messages that resonate with like-minded people who WANT you and what you offer, even though they've never met you. The more you can zone in on these folks, the more you will repel the others. That's simply how it works.

And, the more you repel, the better. The less time you spend on these folks, the more time you can focus on your Ideal Clients. In our experience this will not only increase your sales and repeat sales, but also their lifetime value and the number of quality like-minded referrals just like the ones you've got… with lower cost, less effort and less stress!

We'll expand on this more in Chapter 6 and 7, and show how this approach puts the 80/20 Rule working FOR you, instead of the other way around. But first, let's look at What you do and sell, and how to create the perfect "Strategic-Tactic" that will get you the most results.

CHAPTER 5

So What?

> "In business, everything is subject to change —
> people, products, buildings, machinery, everything
> — except principles. To paraphrase Thomas
> Jefferson, in matters of principle, stand like a rock;
> in other matters, swim with the current."
>
> — MARY KAY ASH

Once you know *Why* they'll buy, and *Who* they are, the next step is to determine *What* you're going to offer them.

Most businesses start out with the *What* or the *Who*, but how do you figure these out if you don't know *Why* you are unique and *Why* you resonate with them? Answering their *Why* means you can now define your *What* by what they really need (and usually want).

Define/Redefine your "What" based on your "Why and Who"

What You Do and **What You Sell** are less important than what your market is looking for. Your Ideal "Who" Client will guide you on "What" to offer and the *Core Message They Need To Hear* to respond.

Your *What* includes things like your product or service, the results or transformation you provide, your price points, your call to action, and your core message to market. Of these, What you offer is less important than the RESULTS or transformation your Ideal Clients will realize by working with or doing business with you.

You are their problem-solver, solution-provider, results-giver — not some hard-selling, feature-benefit, "We're Number One" caricature. **Your Ideal Clients already want you… They just haven't met you or heard about you yet!**

> **Tim adds:** It's not all that hard when you are looking through their eyes, asking them questions about what's driving them. What are you going to offer them that will:

- **REDUCE something that drags them down?**
- **IMPROVE their business?**
- **INCREASE their revenues, quality time, etc.?**
- **SIMPLIFY their life?**

These are by no means the only points your message needs to clearly answer. They need you to connect the dots and tell them more. More than features and benefits, they want to know what it will mean before, during and after the sale, and the consequences of not doing business with you. Your Message is the one "*What*" that straddles the line between **Strategy and Tactics** — *Where, When* and *How* you connect with your Ideal Prospects.

PARETO
PRINCIPLE
20% OF YOUR WORK BRINGS 80% OF THE MONEY
80% OF YOUR SALES COME FROM 20% OF YOUR CLIENTS
80%
20%
80%
20%

CHAPTER 6

Putting The 80/20 Rule to Work FOR You

"Your primary marketing mission is to eliminate as many people as you can, so your message will resonate more with the ones you want the most."

— EMERSON BRANTLEY

The **80/20 Rule** — also known as the **Pareto Principle** — basically states that, in a typical system, we spend 80% of our time, effort and money on those activities and clients that give us only 20% of our results. The reverse is that we only have 20% of our time and resources left for the ones that give us our 80%. For most businesses, the 80/20 is their enemy, not their friend. So, their marketing attracts *some* Ideal Prospects, but a boatload of the other kind — the time-wasters, whiners, complainers, and deadbeats who don't pay, or chargeback when they do.

> "What would your business look like if you spent 80% of your time, efforts and money finding, attracting and nurturing these long-term relationships of value?"

If your focus is the quantity of leads, not their quality, then marketing can bring them in by the thousands. This may work for some businesses, such as affiliate marketing where simply emailing ever-changing offers to mass numbers of people is the goal, not building lifetime customer relationships of value.

But if adding value through your own products or services is your objective, then getting thousands of unqualified leads (the ones you don't want) for your salespeople to deal with makes no sense.

Is it any wonder salespeople HATE wasting time with most of these people? "We can always hire more salespeople to plow through them — we just need better closers!" The result is the Pareto Principle ends up working against your profitability, requiring significant resources to sift, sort and separate the good from the bad AFTER they've responded and are on your list.

What if you could make the Pareto Principle work FOR you instead of against you?

What if you could really eliminate the ones you don't want from the get-go, before they ever respond, so you have more time to spend on the Ideal Clients you want most? What if your marketing could do the job of repelling *AND* attracting? What would your business look like if you spent 80% of your time, efforts and money finding, attracting and nurturing these long-term relationships of value?

You're never going to eliminate all the ones you don't want, but if you can eliminate 80% of them right now, the 20% that's left will be far more likely to have the characteristics and traits you want. Now, the 80/20 rule starts working in reverse - working in your favor - instead of working against you. You can focus 80% on your 20% most qualified, most ready-to-buy — your Ideal Prospects and clients — and start winnowing them down to the 20% of the 20%, your leanest, most profitable vein of revenue. Can you do this in YOUR business?

> "Choosing the right Message, Methods and Channels is key to making the Tactical decisions business owners and entrepreneurs spend most of their marketing efforts trying to figure out."

You can, by using the power of "*Why*" to understand exactly *Who* already wants you, but just doesn't know it yet. At the same time, you will get more clarity on Who *isn't* right for you. Knowing these different groups will help you refine your Message to Market — the words, phrases and "copywriting" that speaks to your Ideal Prospects so clearly and directly that the others "self-exclude" themselves. The more your message is on point for the ones you really want, the more it will repel the ones you don't.

A lot has been written about the *Law of Attraction,* but like Yin and Yang, the *Law of Repulsion* is also your friend. Craft your message to zone in on your Ideal Prospects and you'll get the 80/20 Rule working for you.

In Section Two, we'll delve more into what it takes to develop your Message. We'll also break down the important factors of choosing your **Methods and Channels** to reach your Ideal Prospects. We will discuss the TWO types of key **Referrals** you could be leveraging in a standardized, predictable way. You will discover how tracking your metrics — the hard data that shows how your market is responding to your messaging — along with the powerful effect having a **Marketing+Sales Partnership** brings you, will give you the "soft intel" you need to get better and better with each campaign: *Continuous Improvement!*

American statistician W. Edwards Deming introduced this powerful concept to Japan after WWII. He is widely considered the father of Japan's post-war economy and the way they approach quality. In Japan, the highest award in business is still the Deming Award. There, the concept of continuous improvement is referred to as *kaizen* and applies to every element of business. We'll discuss that in more detail later, in Section Two.

Choosing the right *Message, Methods and Channels* is key to making the Tactical decisions business owners and entrepreneurs spend most of their marketing efforts trying to figure out. We'll cover others as well. Hopefully, you can already see from this first section how, by really getting your *Why* and *Who* down pat, and by only defining your *What* afterwards, all these other tactical decisions will become so much clearer and easier to make.

These two downloads will help clarify what we've covered in this section

Here are additional resources you may download that may be helpful as you develop your own strategies and tactics:

Why-To-Wealth Blueprint™
www.MoreThanStrategy.com

Why-To-Wealth Action Questions™
www.Why2Wealth.com

IT'S LIKE **YIN AND YANG** - THE **LAW OF ATTRACTION** HAS AN OPPOSITE BUT EQUALLY IMPORTANT **LAW OF REPULSION.**

Section Two

TACTICS
(Message, Methods and Channels)

"When marketing answers their objections first, you will always close more sales."

— TIMOTHY R. JOHNSON, CO-FOUNDER OF
THE WHY-TO-WEALTH STRATEGY SYSTEM™

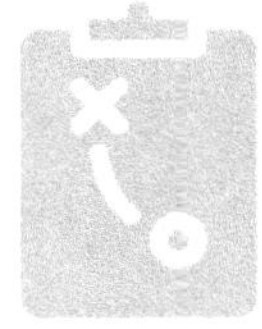

The Critical "Strategic-Tactic" to Reach Your Ideal Prospects

"The methods and channels you choose are only effective to the degree your message is on target."

— EMERSON BRANTLEY, CO-FOUNDER OF
THE WHY-TO-WEALTH STRATEGY SYSTEM™

The blind leading the blind

We've seen how most small businesses and entrepreneurs start with their Tactics. Most marketing training, conferences and consulting revolves around these decisions. Even major international

> "...your *Core Message to Market* comes from understanding exactly Who your Ideal Prospects are, their Whys and how to answer them."

corporations we've worked with spend most of their time focused on the Tactical elements of their marketing, with very little focused on their Strategy.

But as we've seen, the foundation of your marketing — and the decisive element for every tactical decision — is your overall Strategy, that 100,000-foot **Vision and Value** for your business and your market. Your Strategy guides you in determining the exact best **Message, Methods and Channels** to get you the most (and most qualified) Marketing responses, Sales conversions and Lifetime Value from every Ideal Client.

Your Number One Tactic

You may remember that we mentioned your Message is the piece of the puzzle that spans both Strategy and Tactics. That's because your *Core Message to Market* comes from understanding exactly Who your Ideal Prospects are, their *Whys* and how to answer them. As you go through this process, you will begin developing your messaging Strategically.

Your Message also becomes your number one *Tactical* element, because the Methods or Channels you use are of little importance if your Message to Market doesn't match up. Your marketing

Message (or copywriting) is at the center of every single point of contact you have with your Ideal Prospect/Client — every ad, email, video, interview, phone and sales script.

When you get good at this, your copywriting will get better, attracting more Ideal Clients and repelling the less-than ideal. That's exactly what you want to happen — eliminating more of the people you don't want, who don't resonate with you or your message and will never be the Ideal Clients you want the most. Broadcasting a message to these people wastes money. You waste even more money and time dealing with them, trying to "close" the sale by overcoming all their objections. We'll explore how Objections are really Opportunities in Chapter Nine.

How your Why, Who and What help you create your Core Message

Knowing your Who and their Whys should make it easier to create a Message to Market match Message to Market match so precise, when your Ideal Prospects read or hear it they feel almost like you've been reading their diary.

You've already dialed into their inner drivers, and as long as you are **Authentic, Congruent and Consistent,** your message will resonate with the Ideal Prospects

> "…your message should immediately distinguish you from others in your space, repelling the ones you don't want and attracting the ones you do."

you want and they will respond. The clearer your message gets, the more it will connect with these folks, while attracting fewer of the ones you don't want.

And, as your message gets clearer speaking the Why drivers of your Ideal Prospects, it will resonate even less with the ones you don't want. By focusing your message this way and continuously improving it, you will get more of the more highly qualified ones you want for less wasted dollars!

Higher quality leads CAN cost you LESS!

Not only that, your Message is "training" them from the beginning, guiding into a productive, mutually beneficial relationship of value. They are looking for this. Unfortunately, most businesses never take this approach, so they attract clients they don't want and when they try to guide the sales or relationship path, these clients feel like they're being pushed along. Done correctly, your prospects and clients will feel like they're in the arms of a skillful and respectful dance partner, and will follow your lead.

As we discussed earlier, your Message should immediately distinguish you from others in your space, repelling the ones you don't want and attracting the ones you do. The starting point of this process is being totally clear on your own uniqueness. The surest way to do this is to take everything we've talked about up to now and refine it down into the Unique Value Proposition (UVP) that you provide for your Ideal Clients.

Do you have a GREAT Unique Value Proposition? Would you like to?

Your **UVP** (some call it USP, unique selling point or proposition) is that statement that sums up what you do for your Ideal Clients. It requires knowing their *Whys,* **Who** exactly they are (and who they aren't) and the results or transformation they are looking for, the ***What*** you are offering them. When you can answer their *Why* questions, you will discover the unique value you provide that we have... TO your Ideal Clients. Your unique value is not about you — nobody cares! What they care about is the value you're going to bring to them: their "WIIFM?"

Your basic UVP comes down to a simple formula

There are many approaches to creating a powerful UVP. Essentially, the process we've gone through up to now has given you everything you need to have a jaw-dropping, attention-grabbing, eye-opening UVP that clearly states your uniqueness to your Ideal Prospects:

- *Who* **your Ideal Client is**
- **Their** *Why* **— what's driving their decision now?**
- ***What*** **Transformation or Results you provide**

If the people you share your UVP with aren't wowed by it, they're not the ones you want!

Here's a simple formula: telling them exactly Who your Ideal Client is, one of the Big Why issues they struggle with, and What the transformation is you can make happen:

"I help…" — Your Ideal Client

"Who are…" — Whatever it is they're going through - their *Big Why* that's driving them to act

"To…" — The Results or Transformations you deliver. The benefits of choosing you or your company, product or service.

Based on what you discovered in the first section, this should be as precise as possible, so someone who is an Ideal Prospect understands you are who they're looking for.

So, let's use a simple example of someone who is a life coach. If you've been to networking events, it can sometimes seem like there must be more life coaches than people! How can anyone in this arena separate themselves from the pack? At one event, a life coach was introduced to me and when I asked, "What do you do?" she said, "I help women aged 45 to 60 who have been divorced answer the question: 'What's next in my life?'"

So, let's look at what this tells us about her services:

- Does she work with men? No.
- Does she work with women that are going through divorce? No.
- How about 35-year-olds that have been divorced? No.

You immediately know exactly who her Ideal Client is — women aged 45 to 60 who have already been divorced. You know Why they need her and the Big Why that's driving them right now: "I'm 50 years old and solo. What do I do now?" And you know *What* she delivers: Clarity. Answers to help them navigate the rest of their lives.

Most people she meets will respond with, "That's great. Not for me." Or they'll question her or even have some attitude about "Why nots...?". Some may immediately think of someone they can refer who can use her services. But if she's just described you and what you're going through, you immediately feel, "Here's somebody who understands me. Here's somebody who gets me. I've been looking for someone like this. She may have the answers and solutions I need. She's speaking to me in my language. I believe she has what I need."

This one simple statement separated the ones she wanted to work with from the ones who had problems she didn't specialize in. More importantly, she conveyed this with total clarity to her market.

Take a minute and try this yourself. *Who* are you looking for? What are they going through, what is their *Big Why*? And finally, *What* do you deliver?

> "Your brand and position are about relationships, two-way conversations, and the value you bring to your Ideal Prospects and Clients."

Nobody cares *about HOW* you do it. Nobody cares how many buttons, how many bells and whistles, or whatever latest and greatest software, system or technique you have, until they can understand what kind of results it will mean for them (WIIFM?).

It takes more than a great UVP

Your UVP is just the beginning. Your entire Brand Message should build and reinforce this at every touch point. For every Feature, explain the Benefit. Your client should also be clear about the Consequences of *NOT* choosing you. Your message should engage them to respond with, "Tell me more!"

Brand positioning is one of the most misunderstood elements in marketing. To illustrate what we mean, let's consider what a brand is *NOT*:

- A jingle
- A logo, colors or design
- A motto or slogan
- Clever ads
- Cartoon mascots
- Your building, location or signage
- Your trademarks and copyrights

Your Brand and Position ARE about relationships, two-way conversations, and the value you bring to your Ideal Prospects and Clients. Everything you stand for creates the brand your market perceives, and establishes the position you hold in their minds.

Things like honesty, integrity, going the extra mile, providing quality products and services that you back unconditionally wherever possible. Your brand image or logo, your colors and slogans should all reflect this perception, because your market's perception of you *IS* your reality.

When you answer their *Why* drivers satisfactorily, you will have your Unique Value Proposition that clearly defines your brand and positioning — *What* results you provide and precisely *Who* you provide these for. Your number-one focus needs to be establishing you as their one — and only — reasonable choice. In this position, you have zero competition.

> "All your other Tactical decisions, the Where, When and How, are only important and effective if your Message is on target."

Your most important tactical consideration is developing a Core Message your market will respond to, that gets their attention and speaks to them in such a way that you raise their interest and create enough desire that they respond. In marketing and sales this is referred to as **A.I.D.A. — Attention, Interest, Desire and Action.**

All your other Tactical decisions, the *Where, When* and *How*, are only important and effective if your message is on target. Spend most of your Tactical focus and resources on making your message as clear and precise as possible.

SALES FUNNEL 

ATTENTION

INTEREST

DESIRE

ACTION

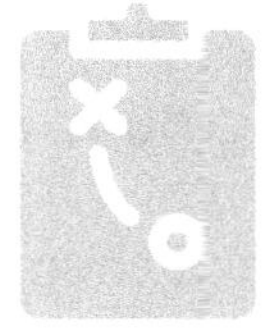

CHAPTER 8

Methods and Channels

*"Most people think 'selling' is the same as 'talking'.
But the most effective salespeople know that
listening is the most important part of their job."*

— ROY BARTELL

Choosing your best Where, When and How Tactics

Your other tactical choices involve the ways you reach your Ideal Clients, your **Methods and Channels.** Your overall **Marketing+Sales Strategy** will guide you to decide which ways are best, based on *Who* they are, their *Why* and your *What*, (your product, service and message). Knowing these, now you can use the **Three Tactical Qualifiers** to make your decisions: **Where, When and How.**

Where are your Ideal Prospects? Where are the best places to find them grouped together? These can be physical places, such as conferences, churches, organizations, political affiliations, ZIP codes, Facebook or LinkedIn groups, etc.

When is the best time to reach them? First thing in the morning, at home, at work, reading an airline magazine, watching the news, driving home, surfing the web, etc.?

How do you reach them? Email, direct mail, Facebook Live, AdWords or SEO when they're browsing, at an event, TV or radio, over the phone, face-to-face, through **Referral Partners** — what are the best ways to get your message in front of them?

Each of these have advantages and disadvantages, depending on your market, product or service. You will often use a combination of these. Your overall Strategy determines how they all fit together to achieve your ultimate Vision.

Can't I have a Facebook, SEO or radio "strategy"?

This is where people get confused the most. The short answer is, each of the Where, When and How choices are all *Tactical.* The bigger answer goes back to the question: **"What's our Strategy?"**

Using social media is not a 'strategy,' it's simply one more Tactic to help you fulfill your overall Marketing Strategy. If using a tactic such as Facebook fits into your overall Strategy, then it belongs. If not, then it doesn't belong. Likewise for search engine optimization (SEO), radio,TV, email or any other Tactical element.

If you recall, this is where we began in Chapter 1: **Strategy comes before Tactics.** In other words, instead of thinking about a 'strategy' to reach a goal, your tactical goals and efforts are only there to achieve your overall Strategy.

Trying to create an separate 'strategy' for each tactic is like the "tail wagging the dog." It usually results in a lot of separate moving parts that can often duplicate or even erase your efforts or worse, confuse what's really working from what's not.

Even some of your products or services — *What* you offer — may be unnecessary, distracting or confusing, diluting the results your overall Strategy should be achieving. Instead of building a 'strategy' around existing products and services, go back to the Why questions. If a product or service doesn't fit, get rid of it. You're your focus on what's working and what other pieces may be needed to fulfill your Ideal Clients' Why drivers instead.

Anything that falls outside of your 100,000-foot **Marketing+Sales Strategy** should be eliminated. So, there cannot be a standalone 'strategy' for Facebook or any other tactical element beyond simply being clear about how it fits into your overall Strategic Vision and Value. This **Why-To-Wealth Strategy System™** makes choosing the right Message, Methods and Channels much simpler. Not only that, your Tactics will all function together in harmony and synergistically, getting you much better results than you will ever experience without using your 100,000 foot Strategy to guide them.

SALES
go
UP & DOWN
SERVICE
STAYS
FOREVER

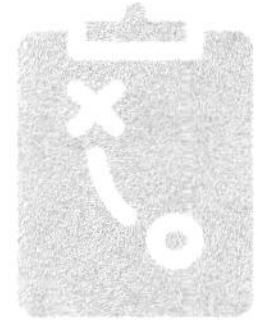

CHAPTER 9

Objections= Opportunities

"Every sale has five basic obstacles: no need,
no money, no hurry, no desire, no trust."

— ZIG ZIGLAR

When you begin using the many different Tactics available, you'll find you can generate an amazing number of leads, often for little or no cost. Since most small businesses and entrepreneurs have never enjoyed consistent lead flow, this is a good thing, right? Lots of leads keep salespeople busy.

If you're speaking to their *Why* drivers, letting them know what solutions and transformations you can provide for them, you'll

> "Objections=
> Opportunities,
> if your sales and
> marketing teams
> work together."

begin attracting more Ideal Prospects. Later in this section, we'll discuss your tracking and metrics, where you can see if your message is hitting the mark or not. For many marketing organizations, getting more traffic and leads is where it ends. In fact, if you talk to as many marketing teams as Tim and I have, you'll hear comments like these:

"We really crushed it this month! Our new campaign surpassed our goals and got us more new leads than ever! Still, no matter how many hot prospects we get in the door, it seems like sales blows through them. Those guys just don't know how to close, or they're just lazy. We're doing all this work and they just keep whining. We need some strong closers who know how to make a sale happen and don't just make excuses for their own low numbers."

> "With strong follow-up programs in place, your customer lifetime value increases, as does the number of quality referrals."

However, when we get the salespeople off to the side, it's a different story:

"Where do the marketing guys get these leads, Craigslist? When we get a live one, we slam-dunk every time, but these people are all bogus, broke and not even in the market. And what about that new campaign? What were they talking about in those ads? All they do is burn daylight over there and waste our time overcoming the same old objections and excuses with non-buyers. We need somebody who isn't in some 'creative coma' to get out there and find us some good ones, fast!"

So far, we've mostly talked about the Marketing side of the **Marketing+Sales Strategy**. Here's where Sales really start to take the lead.

So… Who's to blame?

Neither. Each side blames the other and neither has a real understanding or appreciation of the value each brings to the table. And the fact is *it's not their fault*. This disconnect isn't a people problem, it is a breakdown in the system that only you, the business owner, entrepreneur or CEO, can change. But it takes a real commitment to implement the steps to make it work.

For decades, sales programs have taught salespeople that the key to success is their ability to "overcome objections" by being smarter and cleverer than their buyer. This strategic approach makes customer objections an obstacle course to climb over, burrow under, go around or simply barge through. Prospects and customers have names for salespeople who believe this and practice it: *pushy, aggressive, rude*. Often, these salespeople have a "buy or die" mentality, and potential sales simply fall through the cracks because they're on to the next hot lead or big sale, and their follow-up system is ineffective, inconsistent or nonexistent.

From our experience and personal sales and marketing successes, I believe this is all wrong. **Objections=Opportunities, *IF* your Sales and Marketing Teams Work Together.** When your marketing reaches the *right prospects with the right message*, and can *recognize and address their concerns, doubts and fears upfront*, all Sales needs to do is continue the conversation to bring the prospect to their buying decision. This **Marketing+Sales Strategy** respects your prospect and sees them as a partner in the process, not an adversary defending their credit cards who must be defeated for the sale to happen.

What's missing is a *Partnership* between Marketing and Sales

Marketing — operating alone — can implement everything they know about the Ideal Prospect into their messaging. They can answer all their *Why* questions and reach them right *Where* they are. *When* they are primed and ready to hear your message, using the right Methods and Channels (your *How*) will get it through to them. Marketing can do everything right and still have lots of leads coming through that must be "closed" first.

Sales — also in their own "vacuum" — can overcome objections till the cows come home, and sure, they'll get good at "closing" and everyone will think they're heroes. **What a waste of time and money!**

Marketing may believe they're doing great, hitting big numbers of opt-ins or leads and surpassing goals. But the Sales team is always griping about the quality of the leads and blaming them for their low closing averages. The truth is both sides are working with a handicap. There's no *Partnership* **between Marketing and Sales!**

Your Sales team talks with your customers and new leads and hears the same objections every day. Nothing is more valuable to Marketing than for Sales to share what they know because, with the right information, a trained Marketing team can zero in on the Ideal Prospects you need most. Then, using the **Whytology™ Process Formula** they can continually tweak and refine your message to get even higher quality leads in greater numbers.

With more pre-qualified leads, **your closing averages go up** and **so do your dollars per sale**. With strong follow-up programs in place, **your customer lifetime value increases, as does the number of quality referrals. Establishing a Marketing+Sales Partnership, or MSP, SOLVES this problem!**

We've never done a Strategic "Boardroom" day with any company or entrepreneur that dealt with more than the same 20 or 25 major objections every single day. Usually the SAME ones every day…over and over again!

When business owners and entrepreneurs call us to help them with this process, it's usually because their sales aren't where they want them to be. We can fine-tune your sales team's techniques and boost your numbers through the roof, but that's usually only half the problem.

Emerson adds: "It's not as simple as looking at their 'Frequently Asked Questions' or FAQs on their website to know what their biggest objections or "Big Whys" are. From a marketing perspective, most FAQs are almost worthless because they don't really address the questions in a way that leads to an action or even a gentle trial close.

What if we take what Sales knows and hand it over to Marketing? Maybe Marketing could answer the questions and objections upfront, the same way Sales does on the phone or in person. The better we get at eliminating the issues before they reach Sales, the less they have to deal with the same old questions and objections over and over again. With higher quality leads, Sales spends less time 'closing' while their sales percentages and revenues per customer go up.

The biggest single issue almost always is: Your Marketing and Sales are Disconnected

The solution is to create a *systemized* way for Sales to communicate with Marketing and share the objections they keep running into every day. Sales are on the front line, talking to and listening to prospects and customers day-in, day-out. When we can create a process for them to share what they know with Marketing, your

Marketing team can begin fine-tuning your message to answer these objections, *BEFORE* people respond. We call this process the **Marketing+Sales Partnership, or MSP.**

It's good from a Sales standpoint if I go to Emerson in Marketing and I say, "Emerson, I keep hearing our customers say they're either looking for this or their objection is that. Let's look at how we can circumvent those objections in the marketing Message that we put out." When you listen to your customers, both your programs and your sales are going to improve because you're selling them exactly what it is they're asking for. If the objection is a major one, you will eliminate most of these people from wasting your sales team's time. They will self-exclude themselves. If it's not major (and most objections aren't), your Message can address it upfront, just as a Salesperson would, and you have better prepared the Prospect for their conversation with Sales.

> "When you listen to your customers, both your programs and your sales are going to improve because you're selling them exactly what it is they're asking for."

This isn't a one-time fix!

And it's not simply having casual conversations or hitting a few points in weekly meetings together. Your **Marketing+Sales Partnership** is an ongoing structured system with accountability on all sides. It is worth dedicating the time and focus to set this up properly, as part of your overall Strategy. When done right, you will bridge the gap between Marketing and Sales, and your message will be continuously improved and refined. This will result in more of the most qualified Ideal Prospects you want, and they will be more ready to make a buying decision.

> **Emerson adds:** "Not only that, Tim, but your costs-per-lead actually go down the better we get at delivering that message, because we're more zoned in. This goes counter to everything we've ever heard, right? More qualified leads are supposed to cost you more, not less. It takes some work but when we get this **Marketing+Sales Partnership** in place the opposite happens because Marketing can answer most of their inner *Why* drivers and the objections they create in advance. You end up with better leads for less cost. Tracking metrics and KPIs (Key Performance Indicators) will give you hard data that shows you're on the right track. But only Sales can tell Marketing what the metrics cannot — the "soft" data or intel that the customers are sharing with them, in person or on the phone."

This approach will make every sale easier

When you get this right, your salespeople can literally become "order takers" because your marketing has been able to deliver more of the *RIGHT* prospects, already prepped and positive about you before Sales sits down with them.

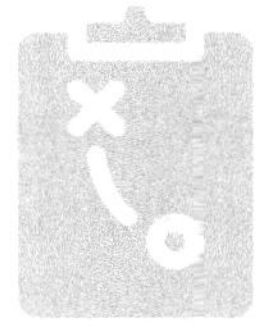

Making the Marketing+ Sales Partnership Work: Continuous Improvement

"Listening offers data. Hearing offers empathy and intelligence. Activity, action, and engagement steer perspective and encourage a sense of community and advocacy."

— BRIAN SOLIS

Creating your **Marketing+Sales Strategy** is the foundation of the **Why-To-Wealth Strategy System™** and the core strength of our proprietary **S.O.L.D. Business Development Process™**.

When you put the powerful **Marketing+Sales Partnership** in place, a transformation begins to happen in your business. By under-standing your Ideal Clients' **Whytology™** — their hidden drivers that compel them to do business with you — *and only you* — you will begin to experience dramatic improvements in your customer acquisition and sales processes that will:

- REDUCE Your Sales Cycle
- IMPROVE Your Sales Per Lead
- INCREASE Your Revenues Per Customer
- SIMPLIFY Your Sales Process

Just like Marketing must understand your Ideal Clients' *Why,* Sales must too.

If your Sales team is stuck on being "smarter and cleverer" than the prospects they're talking to, even when Marketing drives in your Ideal Prospects, they will still put up a strong resistance. Instead of being smart, I coach salespeople to **"stay stupid!"** Ask lots of questions, speaking in "You" language that engages your prospect and reveals their *Why* — the innermost feelings, thoughts, habits, and patterns that **drive them** to make that buying decision... or convince them not to.

> "When you put the powerful **Marketing+Sales Partnership** in place, a transformation begins to happen in your business."

Ask yourself, do you or your team use lots of "I" statements instead of "YOU" statements? You know, "I can do this..." "We can handle that..." "Our program is better because..." After the first two or three, if you haven't hit their underlying *Why* drivers, you're just making noise, and your prospects will shut you down.

When we use "I" statements like "I do this" and "I do that" we sound like a bad date...when ultimately, what we should be talking about is how it benefits them. What's the problem that your product that your product or service is going to solve for them?

That's what is going to get them to spend the money they want to spend. People will spend a lot more money on pain than they will on pleasure. To put it another way, if they have no problems, why would they spend the money to fix what isn't broken? For you to be their problem-solver, they must have a problem to solve.

Here's how this plays out when you've taken the time to **build your Marketing and Sales Strategies together**, not based on you, but based on your Ideal Prospects' *Whys*, and you are willing to be a little stupid. Whenever you talk with a prospective buyer, they're expecting a sales pitch, but what I'm looking for is to benchmark *where they are today, where they want to be in three to five years and what challenges they need to overcome to get there?*

There are three — and only three — kinds of objections you need to address:

- Is their challenge about finding *Time?*
- Is it about *Money?*
- Or is it about *Change?*

Remember, they've been over-promised and under-delivered their entire life. Why should they believe you're any different if you don't even know their *Why* — or care enough to ask?

Can you show them how to save **Time**, or free it up? Or can you show them how to add your program or product into their already full schedule and make it work? How much time do they have? How much do they need?

When Money is an objection to your price, it simply means you haven't given them enough value, or their issue isn't big enough. How much is "too expensive" when they see your solution solving a pressing problem in their life? It's up to Sales to find out, and show them the ROI (return on investment) that justifies their decision. They will find the funds if the value is clear. Even if your product or service increase their income or revenues, or save them taxes or other losses, none of these are enough of a reason to buy. A lot of people will tell you they want more Money, but that's not their real WHY. If they haven't told you Why they want it, exactly what does "having more money" mean to them? And how much is "more"? It's up to us to find out.

We all hate **Change**. It can increase stress, frustration and give us new problems to deal with. What we have now may not be perfect, but it's easier to stick with what we've got rather than struggle through a new learning curve. That's why there are still people using old, outdated software like Windows 98 — or older!

These three core objections are all related to each other. We can show you how to make more money, but is it truly going to give you more time or make a drastic difference to your lifestyle? Will it create more headaches for you to make the change, or simplify your life and reduce your stress? Most of the time, your answers won't be about you but whatever you care about most — like your family, your employees or your legacy.

Ask probing questions like, "What have you tried up until now?" "What programs do you have already?" "How have they worked for you?" "Are your decisions based on costs? Fear of loss? Hope of gain?" "How has accountability (or lack of) played into your results (or lack of) so far?"

Maybe your *Why* is to make more money so you can put your kids through college. Maybe it's to reduce stress and pay off debt, to be able to travel, or enjoy the lifestyle you deserve. Maybe it's making a nest-egg to ensure your golden years are covered. For entrepreneurs or business owners, ask questions like, "What specifically, growth wise, would you use the money for?" "How would that affect your P&Ls, your bottom line?"

> **Emerson adds:** "We're guiding them to *Why* they've made the decisions they've made and owning the consequences of their decisions. What are their consequences if they DON'T do this? What are the consequences if they fail... for them, their business, family, employees, future, etc.? It's sort of like being married. If you've been married two, three, four times or more, at some point you have to quit the blame game — look at yourself and ask, 'What was driving those choices?'"

As Marketing and Sales both get better at understanding your Ideal Clients' *Why* drivers, it makes it easier to transport them from today's reality into their future possibilities, and to help them really understand what it means to them if they don't act now.

"What's the impact in your life if you don't do this?" "What's it going to cost you over your lifetime, not to make these changes just because you've been overpromised and under-delivered in the past?" "What does your future look like, living another day, another month, another year, or three, or five, or longer, without having achieved the results you really want?"

You can call these pain points, fears, frustrations or problems, but this process is all about getting them to honestly look at the consequences of *NOT* making this buying decision, now.

Sales is only part of the solution

Marketing can take the "soft" intel from Sales and fine-tune their Message to Market, then monitor their hard data metrics again to see if they're on point. Then they use the **Marketing+Sales Partnership or MSP** and share their results with Sales, to see if the tweaks and changes are making a difference in the conversations Sales are having. They've got to start working together. It starts with Marketing, but they can only take the ball so far. It takes the entire team to get all the way down the field and they only manage it when there is a strong **Marketing+Sales Partnership** in place.

It's not just a one-person or one-department show. **Your Feedback Loop becomes the energy that drives quantum growth.** Without it, their **Objections** never become the *Opportunities* they could be, to continuously improve what you do and achieve greater results. Not only that, sometimes their Objections will guide you into new products and services you may not have even considered... or help you improve the ones you have to better fit what your market is telling you they really want.

In the next chapter, we'll talk about what to do with all those prospects who still respond but for whatever reason, aren't the right fit — not right now anyway. We'll look at how you can monetize them with **Referral Partners**, and get more of your Ideal Clients to endorse you to others.

Later, we'll talk about how to **Duplicate and Automate** your workflows, so your business will be more profitable with less effort and stress, enjoying higher-qualified *Ideal Prospects* for less cost per lead or sale than you are likely spending now. Plus, we'll cover how to create a "second tier" for your **Referral Partners**, to be able to refer them and to make it easy for them to refer you, so you can begin creating that "Mailbox Money" that Tim is so fond of building into businesses.

> "It starts with Marketing, but they can only take the ball so far. It takes the entire team to get all the way down the field and they only manage it when there is a strong **Marketing+Sales Partnership** in place."

AT FIRST
THEY WILL ASK
WHY
YOU'RE DOING IT
LATER THEY'LL ASK
HOW
YOU DID IT

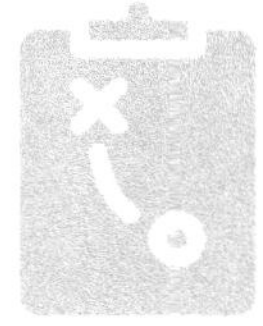

CHAPTER 11

Leveraging Referrals

"In the business of referrals, trust is the most important reason a recommendation is made and, conversely, lack of trust the single greatest reason referrals don't happen."

— JOHN JANTSH

The easiest prospect of all

Common sense and experience in sales tells us that the most difficult sale is the cold call. The prospect doesn't know you, isn't expecting you and may or may not be interested when you call them. None of us like unsolicited calls interrupting our dinner, right? This is the oldest, most challenging and time-consuming way to get customers, and while it was effective in the distant past, there are too many better ways to get business today that engage prospects instead of accosting them. The second-most difficult sale is the outbound call to a warm lead or prospect. At least, in these cases, the salesperson has a connection with someone who has indicated interest in what is being sold at some point.

Inbound, or customer-initiated responses are much, much easier and smoother. The prospect has chosen to take the moment to reach out and say, "Tell me more." They are not looking for a hard sell but inviting a conversation to get information they are interested in. They believe you just might have the solution they need, and are ready to talk.

The best, easiest and by far the most valuable prospects to talk with are direct referrals, where you have been endorsed by someone they trust. It's best if they are calling you or being introduced directly by a current Ideal Client, but even if you reach out to them, they are already primed and interested.

> **Emerson adds:** "In our marketing, we may create campaigns to cold or warm lists or groups, but when we do joint ventures or endorsed campaigns, we can always expect higher results. The more they know and trust the person referring or endorsing us, the greater our results will be. Trust and confidence are major *Why* issues, and when they feel they can trust the recommendation, they feel they can trust us as well. The entire sales conversation changes when trust isn't an issue."

For most small businesses and entrepreneurs, getting referrals is an afterthought, and sometimes not even a first thought. At best, the salesperson may push a list over to them, ask for referrals or offer some "bird dog" payment for anyone they recommend. Sure, people like a little extra cash, but most people they refer to you well, because they believe in you and know you'll treat referrals well, that they won't be embarrassed or sorry they sent you business.

This lack of focus on a strong referral system is too bad, since **getting more qualified referrals is the fastest, surest and easiest way to quantum leap your business revenues**. Imagine if each of your Ideal Clients referred others like themselves. Over the course of a year, if these referrals resulted in just one new client each, you have effectively doubled your business before spending a dime on finding new Ideal Prospect leads.

So, how do you get more referrals from your Ideal Clients?

You may recall one of the purposes of your Message is to begin to "train" prospects on what you expect from your Ideal Clients. In other words, you are looking for relationships, not just sales numbers. Relationships have expectations, and from the very first contact you should be telegraphing your expectations. One of the early expectations is that, once you help solve their issue, fulfill their need and give them the results they are looking for — in other words, once you have over-delivered on your "under-promises" — and they see you are the real deal, you expect them to *"pay it forward"* and share their experience with others.

You will have NO resistance at this stage of the process, because you are only describing an action for them to take once they have seen how you deliver on your promises. Remember, they've been over-promised and under-delivered many times before. It doesn't matter that in their minds, they're likely thinking, "Sure, not a problem if they deliver, but they might be the same as all the others." What's important is you've set up the expectation, and gotten a conditional commitment you can remind them of later on. Can you see the power of positioning referrals this way, as an expectation of the type of relationship, not as a request to "gimme some names"? When you deliver value, they will reciprocate beyond the dollars paid in the form of additional referrals and revenues.

Partner Referrals

We've seen how, when Marketing gets feedback from the Sales team about what they're running into, they can fine-tune your Message and make it clearer, so that the people coming through to Sales are more of the right people and less of the wrong ones. Sales get to work less to sell more. Even when your marketing is doing everything right, and your **Marketing+Sales Partnership** is creating Continuous Improvement in the number and quality of your leads, some prospects will still not be the right fit.

> "Relationships have expectations, and from the very first contact you should be telegraphing your expectations."

They may simply not be ready for what you offer yet. There may be other decisions to be made or other things they need in place first. It could be timing, budgetary limitations, a legacy relationship with another provider, being locked into their company's RFB guidelines (request for bid) and lowest-price requirements, or any one of a hundred other things. That's okay. We remind our clients to refer to our SW4 Formula:

**Some Will.
Some Won't.
So What?
Someone's Waiting!**

This keeps your focus on-track and eliminates feeling the need to revert to old-school, "cleverer" processes to try to force a sale. If it's not the right fit, don't sell them something they don't need. All those people we don't want could still be clients of other companies we know of, who have what they need, and that creates a whole second cycle where we're talking about **Referral Partners**.

BE the Solution Provider they are looking for!

Who are the people that your Idea Clients need? What products or services do they use or are they trying to find? What other things do they need to Improve, or maybe Reduce? What do they need to Increase? What could be Simplified and made easier for them?

Who can you put them with to provide other products or services they need?

We created **Whytology™** because the more you understand what your clients need and what they want, and know how to speak it, do you really have to sell them? No, you don't. Because I know who I'm not for, I just connect those people with my **Referral Partners**.

So, if you need funding assistance, we have that. Merchant account for processing credit cards? Got it. Someone to automate your online customer acquisition and sales? Yep. Get your Message to Market on target? No problem. Help you get a book written like this one and promote you as a celebrity in your field? Absolutely. Create endless, effortless testimonials and five-star ratings? Have it. Or, more precisely, we have a trusted **Referral Partner** who specializes in what you need.

We've spent years developing these relationships. We've tested them and, in most cases, use them every day. If you understand your Ideal Prospects and Clients, it's simple to upsell them to the people they need because you're not doing anything too complicated. You're just sharing information they need in a way that they'll gratefully receive it. Now, here's the key — don't just send an email that says, "Ted meet Joan, Joan meet Ted." Have a system that streamlines the process. We'll talk more about how to **Duplicate and Automate** your systems in the next chapter. For now, figure out four or five things you can say that let's your prospect know that your trusted Referral Partner has what they need. For example, my **Referral Partners** say I'm an expert on:

- **REDUCING Your Sales Cycles**
- **IMPROVING Your Sales Per Lead**
- **INCREASING Your Revenues Per Customer**
- **SIMPLIFYING Your Sales Process**

When they refer Emerson, they tell people he can:

- **REDUCE Their Lead Cost**
- **IMPROVE Their Lead Quality**
- **INCREASE Their Profitability**
- **SIMPLIFY Their Entire Marketing Process**

So, think about what you do for your customers. Think about each person or business you rely on, who have proven themselves to you and may be right for the people in your market as well. Talk with them about a reciprocal relationship, where you get paid for new customers you send them and vice versa. Once you standardize this and automate it, you'll have what I call **"Mailbox Money"** from simply making those introductions.

Can you see how this will supplement your sales to your clients? Not only can you generate **Mailbox Money** from those prospects who don't end up buying from you, you can become a valuable referral resource for your Ideal Clients as well. When they need help, they'll know they can call on you and you'll direct them to someone they can trust, generating revenue without doing any of the work. Plus, your **Referral Partners** will begin recommending you as well. Remember what we said earlier — the easiest sales are referrals.

When we have all of this together, you will have your **Marketing+Sales Strategy** in place. Your **Objections** will be creating new **Opportunities** because of your **Marketing+Sales Partnership**. You'll be seeing regular referrals and extra revenue because you have leveraged your **Referral Partners** and standardized your Ideal Client referrals.

The last part of the **S.O.L.D.**™ **Process** is to **Duplicate and Automate** all of this, so you have an entire money-making system doing all the heavy lifting for you — and that's next!

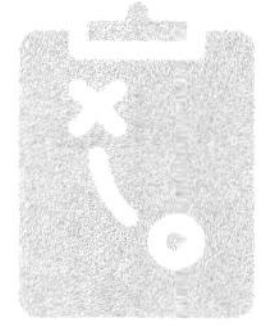

CHAPTER 12

Duplication and Automation

> "Without data you're just another
> person with an opinion."
>
> — W. EDWARDS DEMING

Almost every tactical aspect of the **Sales+Marketing Strategy** can be duplicated, repurposed and reapplied for different products, services and campaigns, once you have established your *Why, Who* and *What*. As you fine-tune your **Message** using the power of your **Marketing+Sales Partnership or MSP,** you'll be able to repurpose and reuse it in different ways and in different media. Using a Customer Relationship Management (CRM) software program is mission-critical to your success, for several reasons.

First, you eliminate time-consuming manual entry and reentry, sending emails and doing follow-ups.

> "When a Referral Partner gives them your referral link, it starts a unique chain of contacts and events to ensure you get the greatest possible chance to "Wow!" them and develop a long-term relationship of value."

Second, you standardize your process, so even though prospects will come into your world at different times, from different places and with different interests and needs, your system is able to handle them as individuals. When a **Referral Partner** gives them your referral link, it starts a unique chain of contacts and events to ensure you get the greatest possible chance to "Wow!" them and develop a long-term relationship of value.

Third, nobody falls through the cracks. When a team returns from a tradeshow with hundreds of leads, it can mean days or weeks of irregular follow-ups. A systemized follow-up system using your CRM means they all get an initial touch right away and, based on responses, can be funneled into different follow-up sequences that meet their needs and interests. It frees up your sales team to spend 80% of their efforts on the 20% who are most engaged.

Fourth, it makes it easy to connect anyone to your **Referral Partners**, rather than just sharing information and hoping something happens. You can use their mobile phone to text into a partner's referral information sequence, and they are instantly connected to receive additional information, links or to set up an appointment for further conversation. In each of these cases, every touch point is tracked right from the source, through every action they take, so you have a clear picture of what is happening in real time, and know what's working and what isn't.

Testing, Tracking and Tweaking

One thing we always advise our clients is to "never stop testing". Every chance you get, challenge your best performing email, ad, landing page, webinar, sales letter or any other parts of your marketing with an alternative. Then watch the difference in your results.

When you test, don't make lots of changes. Stick with one, like your offer or call to action, your price point, headline, the testimonial used, whether a video was included or not, etc. This way, you can see the effect of each element. If you test a lot of different things at once, say the subject line, opening paragraph, price, etc., even if you have greater results, you won't know why.

Your CRM can show you a massive amount of information about how effective your marketing is. Hard data such as email delivery

> "Continuous improvement — or *kaizen* in Japanese — is the idea that systems can never be 100% perfected, so you can continue to get better results as you continue to fine-tune your processes."

rates, open rates, click-throughs, visitors, page views, time on a page, opt-ins, video views, how long they watch, when they leave, downloads and dozens of other Key Performance Indicators or KPIs can help guide you — or overwhelm you. Staying on top of this data is key to fine-tuning your marketing efforts, and it's a good idea to have one person committed to monitoring and reporting your results to you every day. You can read a lot into the numbers when you know what to watch out for.

So, when it comes to **Testing, Tracking and Tweaking**, we can certainly give you some of the most important key metrics to watch as you test different variations of your message. But remember, these are all hard metrics and what I really want to focus on is the *soft intel:* The soft metrics that Sales is getting as objections. Your team is hearing the same objections repeatedly, and this information needs to be conveyed to Marketing through your **Marketing+Sales Partnership or MSP** process, along with ways they have successfully dealt with each issue up to now.

Marketing then tweaks your Message to address these concerns. In some cases, this means satisfying prospects ahead of time so there's no longer an issue — or less of one — by the time they end up talking with your sales team. For example, if your offer involves a high-value product or service, paying the full amount upfront may be a regular stumbling block. Letting the prospects know you can take incremental payments could satisfy their doubts, even without detailed information about your payment program.

In other cases, this may mean stressing the qualifications expected of your Ideal Prospects and Clients. For example, in a national credit investor program, one qualification (or delimiter) was having a minimum credit score of 650, as well as a household income of $70,000 or more. As the Message became more fine-tuned, the response was so great that ***we increased the requirements to limit the responses*** to prospects with greater household income and better credit, and so ended up with fewer responders but ones that were easier and quicker to close and process. In every case, once the soft data is used to tweak the **Message**, the hard data begins telling you the kind of responses you're getting. Then using the **Marketing+Sales Partnership or MSP** Process, Sales lets you know you're getting more of the right people and any other adjustments you need to make.

Continuous improvement

Continuous improvement — or ***kaizen*** in Japanese — is the idea that systems can never be 100% perfected, so you can continue to get better results as you continue to fine-tune your processes. W. Edwards Deming taught that any production line — any system or process — begins and ends with the customer. Rather than go for the impossible goal of "100% defect-free", he used statistical methods to show the Japanese that ***Continuous Improvement*** was the bigger goal.

"kai" means "change" and "zen" means "better."

The statistical inability to reach 100% of your market or get 100% results isn't a bad thing. It means that, no matter how good your marketing and sales teams get, you can always be improving your results and increasing revenues, by testing new concepts, tracking your numbers and tweaking your messaging. So, when we are marketing, we are constantly challenging our "champion" campaigns with new tests, watching our metrics to see what works, what doesn't, and what works better, paying close attention to our customers through our **Marketing+Sales Partnership**. In Sales, we become better listeners, seeing every new Objection or concern as another Opportunity for more improvement in the process.

In this way, all marketing begins by understanding your Ideal Prospects' *Whys* and ends with long-term relationships of mutual value with your Ideal Clients.

These two downloads will help clarify what we've covered in this section

Here are additional resources you may download that may be helpful as you develop your own strategies and tactics:

Why-To-Wealth Blueprint™
www.MoreThanStrategy.com

Why-To-Wealth Action Questions™
www.Why2Wealth.com

Conclusion

"In any moment of decision, the best thing you can do is the right thing. The worst thing you can do is nothing."

— THEODORE ROOSEVELT

A book can do marvelous things. It can open your eyes to new ideas and concepts, alter the way you think and possibly, even change the entire course of your life or business. What makes the difference? Not the book itself — it reads the same for everyone. It's what you DO with the wisdom and insights it offers that matters most. We began this journey with the apparently simple question, "Why?" Now you can see how this one question opens the doors of possibility for your business to go from a commodity, an also-ran average within a pack of other options, to becoming your Ideal Prospects' unique provider, their one-and-only, top-of-the-mind choice.

Exactly *Who they are and Who they aren't*; these are choices most businesses never really address. This one step will save you hundreds, even thousands of dollars, maybe more. When you focus your Message on answering their *Whys* so clearly, you repel the

> *"With these elements firmly in place, you now have a much greater chance of branding and positioning yourself as your market leader, regardless of any other providers in your market space."*

ones you don't want and get more of the ones you do. What you sell and What you say comes next. So often, the *What* is the starting point for small businesses, and especially entrepreneurs. Now you know the *What* is irrelevant until you know the *Who* you're speaking and selling to, and their inner *Why* drivers. Together, these create a Crystal Clear Strategy — a 100,000-foot vision and the Unique Value you offer your Ideal Prospects and Clients.

The *Where*, *When* and *How* Tactical questions should all be much easier now, once you've got your Strategy clear. Can you see how we could say your Tactics are irrelevant, except when they're a part of your overall Strategy? With these elements firmly in place, you now have a much greater chance of branding and positioning yourself as your market leader, regardless of any other providers in your market space.

Is the journey worth it?

We must all make decisions about three things in life: Time, Money and Change. Of the three, some believe Money is the biggest challenge, others Time, but it's Change that's the most difficult of all.

If all this book does for you is open your eyes to the points you're missing or not considering in your marketing and sales efforts, it's well worth you reading it. If all it does is help you get clarity on who your Ideal Client is, so your marketing can be more precise, more cost-effective and bring you better results, that also makes it worth reading.

Even if all it does for you is highlight the importance of your marketing and sales teams coordinating their efforts and sharing what they know with each other to take your marketing to the next level, then it's worth it. However…

Getting the most out of this book requires *Action*

Knowledge itself isn't power. "Shelf help" and filed knowledge cannot impact your life or your business. Only *applied* knowledge makes any difference. Unfortunately, the longer you delay taking decisive action on knowledge, experience and insights, the less effective it will be for you and the fewer results you will see. Just as bad, the results you do receive will come slower and lost opportunities will continue to accrue. So, immediate application of what this book has revealed should be a top priority. Here are the Action Steps we recommend.

Set aside a full day to brainstorm and develop your Strategy… your 100,000-foot Vision and Value that will guide you in every decision

Continue to drill down to fine-tune your definitions of **WHY** and **WHO**, get crystal clear on your Strategic Vision and answer those all-important *Why* drivers in the minds of your Ideal Prospects that clarify your Unique Value. Use what we've talked about in this book as a starting point.

Then, using your Strategy as your guide, review your **WHAT** — your product, service and core message — and make sure it all fits. Start creating your "Copy Bank" of Features, Benefits, Headlines, Stories for your emails and other media, Offers, Calls to Action and everything you need for your campaigns. This is an ongoing process, but you can "jump-start" it by dedicating a second full day focused only on your copywriting.

WHAT product or service offerings make the most sense based on what your Ideal Clients care about most (WIIFM)? What message points will speak to them in ways that will compel them to respond? What does your primary customer path look like? What do your Ideal Prospects respond to, and what are their next-step options in your product mix? Keep what's good, eliminate what's not needed and add the missing pieces your Ideal Prospects want and need.

Next, look at all your Tactical options, the best Methods and Channels to get your Message out there. Be open to considering all viable *Where, When* and *How* options, not just the ones you've always used before or the cheapest ones. Ask yourself these questions:

WHERE are your prospects? Where can you get your message through in the most efficient and effective way possible? Who has the list you need? Who are the influencer companies, groups or individuals you can go into a joint venture with or find lookalike prospects? Are there trade shows, associations or other options where you can reach many at one time? What other factors need to be considered? Are there gatekeepers to get around? What message do they need to hear?

WHEN is the best time to reach them? Are there better times of the year, quarter, season or even days of the week when they are easier to reach, or thinking about the solutions you offer? Are there time issues or fiscal planning dates to consider?

HOW is the best way to reach them? Which channels — online or offline — will have the greatest chance of getting your message to them, so they will notice, pay attention and possibly respond? Are there professional or industry publications they read? Do they gather at conferences or attend seminars or workshops? Are they members of certain LinkedIn or Facebook groups? Are there direct mail, email or solo ad options to reach them? Does your product or service mix appeal to a wider audience that may respond to mass marketing efforts as well? Where could targeted, direct-response PR be most effective?

> "In every case, the cost of inaction is much greater than the short-term time and financial investment of engaging this process now."

We recommend you set aside and dedicate an entire day to fleshing out these kinds of details as one of the most important next steps you could take. At the same time, you will need to further develop your core Brand Message and Positioning, fine-tuning your Unique Value Proposition.

From our experience, we know when you take these actions on what we've shared the effect on your business will be transformative.

In our "Boardroom" Strategy Days we guide this process to map out everything, so you can hit the ground running. Our Copywriting "Boardroom" helps you create your core message and build a powerful "Copy Bank" you can immediately utilize for all your marketing. Regardless of your other needs, chances are we have anything you could possibly need in our extensive "rolodex" to get your program up and running sooner, rather than later.

The Cost of Inaction

What if you choose to simply think about what we've discussed, to chew on it and maybe take a few of the ideas and suggest them to your team? We ask that you consider that.

"If you keep on doing what you've been doing, you'll keep on getting what you've already got."

If having more of the same is what you want, then toss this book and keep on keeping on. In our experience, the cost of not taking direct action and doing the necessary Strategic Planning can include things that are hard to quantify, like delayed market expansion and *lost client opportunities*, not to mention *lost growth and revenues*, and *defaulting market leadership* to your competition. Some things are easier to recognize, like money lost on wasteful, unprofitable marketing campaigns, lengthy sales processes costing unnecessary time and effort, and customers lost through the cracks because of no systemized follow-ups and more.

In every case, the **Cost of Inaction** is many times greater than the short-term time and financial investment of engaging this process now. Based on thousands of clients over the years, when you take immediate action, you shorten your time-to-market curve dramatically and get laser-focused on the fastest new revenue streams you can develop, sooner rather than later. So just do it!

Immediate Action Will Guarantee Different Results

Your action is what will make the difference, and the action you choose will determine whether you experience results that come slowly, quickly or at lightning speed. In every opportunity, we have the same basic choices when it comes to improving the quality of our lives or the profitability of our businesses:

1. **Slowest: Do it yourself (DIY).** This can mean you or your team but essentially, it is the concept of jumping out a plane and learning to make a parachute on the way down, hoping you get enough of it right that you don't crash. You and your team make your best efforts using what you already know. This means the lowest investment in your business, and generally results in the lowest and slowest ROI for all your "sweat equity" efforts.

    It is impossible in a short book like this or, for that matter, any singular book or course, to give you the depth of understanding you need to run your business. Even more importantly, trying to create significant change when you have never gone through the process before is very difficult.

We've all read the statistics about the huge number of businesses that fail within three to five years.

Many reasons are offered for why so many businesses fail, but in our experience, a major part of the problem is the false belief that if you just keep doing whatever it takes, somehow it will all work out. Even when new information or knowledge is brought in, it is impossible not to "filter" it through your own previous knowledge, and that's the root of the problem. You may want to consider this observation from one of the great analytical minds of all time. To paraphrase Albert Einstein, "The significant problems we have cannot be solved at the same level of thinking with which we created them" Or, to put it another way...

"If what you know could get you to where you want to go, you'd already be there."

2. **Fastest: Have it done FOR you (DFY).** At the other end of the spectrum is to have it all done for you. This is by far the fastest path to success, and often leads to growth — doubling, tripling, even three-figure percentages year-on-year. Business owners, CEOs and entrepreneurs who understand true ROI also understand that the "get it done" approach will take your business to the next level in a far more accelerated path than any other method. People can be trained, new ones hired, but revenue growth doesn't wait for anything.

Only a small percentage of small businesses and entre-preneurs have the level of belief and confidence in their offerings, uniqueness and other factors to understand the value of "kick-starting" their business **Strategy and Tactics** this way. The upfront investment may be daunting to some, but the accelerated growth curve more than offsets it with much faster and greater returns on investment. Often, by getting the key steps in place sooner rather than later, team members are brought up to speed faster. Where additional team members or outside players are needed, seeing the growth happening attracts the higher quality that accelerates your growth even faster.

Also, by having the right **Strategists and Tacticians** in place, even the most rapid growth can be scaled in such a way that your business is able to handle it. In our experience, annual growth of 1500-2000% has been realized in some cases. Businesses and entrepreneurs not experienced in this kind of exponential growth can be overwhelmed without the assistance and guidance of someone who has experienced rapid growth many times before.

3. **Fairly Quickly: Do it With A Mentor or Coach Who Has the Knowledge You Need (Done with you, or DWY).** For many small business owners and entrepreneurs, this is the "Goldilocks" option. You and your people are probably capable of taking your business to the next level with the specialized knowledge and experience of someone who has "been there and done that" before. This mentorship, coaching, guidance — call it what you will — can equip and lead you and your people through the process, getting you there faster and with more certainty than the DIY approach. And,

when specific involvement is needed on certain projects, you have someone you can trust who knows your business, your Strategy and who's been integral to your actual planning process, so when the campaign or project is completed, it fits into your entire plan.

This is also the common investment level for businesses where "growing too fast" isn't the goal but building something you can scale is preferred. The Done With You approach will create a greater ROI faster, while equipping you and your people with the right coaching and mentoring to help them grow into their roles to support your future growth.

What's the best approach for you?

The choices you make are entirely dependent on your business, your vision and your market. Often, it's been said the most important element in any success is decisiveness. Indecisiveness is deadly, especially in today's fast-moving business environment. Don't put it off or procrastinate. No decision is a decision. We believe you are of the more decisive mindset, otherwise you wouldn't have this book in your hands in the first place. Here are some questions that it may help to ask yourself as you make your decision.

- What do you want to accomplish?
- Will you be satisfied if you don't?
- Why are you wanting to do this now?
- How will you measure it?
- How fast do you want to get there?
- How important is it to you?

- What steps have you taken so far?
- Why do you need to do anything different?
- What would a reasonable return on your investment be to get there?
- What are the consequences if you don't act now?

Ultimately, the course of action you choose depends on your clarity about the results you want to achieve, and how much investment your vision and dreams are worth.

We suggest you don't limit yourself to experts within your market niche. Often, the solutions they will give you will be nothing more than "monkey see, monkey do".

The **Strategy and Tactics** you need require thinking outside of the box and cross-pollinating ideas from other markets and other areas. It's hard to be unique in your space if you're doing what everyone else is doing. Also, choosing the most qualified expert isn't best done with a "low bid" approach. Instead, talk with them and see if there's a fit, a chemistry. In your first conversation, you will often get a feel for whether they "get" you and your vision and, more than that, if they can see opportunities and possibilities you may not be seeing yourself. Listen to the questions they ask — that's how you know they can take you from where you are now to where you want to go and deliver the results you want.

Types of Client Relationships — How Growth Partners Work

Finding a growth partner is helpful, regardless of which approach you take. There are times when even "Do It Yourselfers" need some input and assistance. While different companies and individuals have various expertise and programs, most offer similar options such as marketing reviews, various analyses and other options. Some offer fewer options than others, so we will use the options we provide as examples.

Boardroom Planning Days

This level of in-depth, Strategic Planning and Message Development days is the fastest way to jump-start your program or restart your marketing and sales if your current efforts aren't performing the way you want. These are intense, focused sessions designed to drill down and get total clarity on your *Why*, the *Why* drivers of your market, *Who* your market is and isn't, and *What* your best offerings and messages should be. To prepare for your Boardroom Day, you will receive our **Comprehensive S.W.O.T. Audit identifying your *Strengths, Weaknesses, Market Opportunities* and *Threats***. This requires your focus and time to complete.

At the end of a Boardroom Day, your entire model will be mapped out to ensure the most profitability and long-term growth, including what to keep, what to eliminate and the people, products or services, and the exact Message you need to achieve your Strategic Goals. *Where*, *When* and *How* to reach your Ideal Prospects and other Tactical options are also mapped out.

Strategic S.W.O.T. Analysis, Ranking & Action Steps

Similar to the Comprehensive S.W.O.T. Audit included in our Boardroom Days, this option gives even "do-it-themself" business owners and entrepreneurs a scaled-down way to get the guidance you need. After our team evaluates and scores your strengths, weaknesses, market opportunities and threats you will receive a written Analysis of our results. Your Analysis includes your numerical Success Ranking as well as specific Action Steps so you can focus your energies and resources to improve your Marketing and Sales efforts. You can find more information on this option at **www.Why2Wealth.com**.

Coaching and Mentoring

Probably the most popular option, this provides you and your team expert guidance, Mentoring and Coaching. While most small businesses and entrepreneurs choose bi-weekly group coaching, for clients who qualify we also offer one-on-one programs customized for you and your company's unique needs. In both cases, we start the relationship with our **Strategic S.W.O.T. Analysis and Review**, so our Coaching and Mentoring can focus on your specific needs, even within the group setting. One thing to consider with any Coaching and Mentoring program is that it will only be effective with a commitment of time over a period of several months. One or two hit-or-miss sessions won't have nearly as much effect. We recommend a six-month minimum to allow time to review, analyze and develop your marketing program together.

Retained Clients

For longer-term relationships, it is always more beneficial to establish a fixed monthly retainer, because it better addresses the scope of your vision and needs and provides an easy-to-budget, "no surprises" monthly amount. Monthly fixed retainers vary depending on the scope and intensity of the marketing required in an average month, and success fees involved.

This option gives you the most value and fastest ROI by completely addressing your specific Strategic and Campaign Development needs. We start with an onsite Boardroom Day for you and your team to clarify your **Marketing+Sales Strategy** and identify the best Tactics to achieve your objectives. Our team also works directly on your Messaging to create dynamic, compelling copywriting and scripting, and directly guide any necessary creative, technical or media services required.

> "Every path chosen involves some level of investment of Time, Money or Change."

Although terms may vary, we recommend a six-month minimum initial contract term to allow us time to ramp up and create initial marketing pieces, launch initial tests, and develop clear go-ahead strategies, benchmarks and solid expectations of the degree of success we will achieve. Very few qualified, experienced experts will work based on sales results alone. Most will require some monthly minimum, especially in the beginning of the relationship. However, a sure mark of a competent and knowledgeable expert provider is their willingness to include a "success fee" as part of their overall compensation.

Success fees are agreed-upon in advance based on your individual products, pricing, markets and sales. They range from 36 months to perpetuity and, at least in our case, is designed to ultimately replace the retainer altogether as quickly as possible. This allows your program to pay for itself with Continuous Improvement of campaign results throughout the contract.

Strategic Mastermind Alliance

A select number of clients are invited to join our Strategic Mastermind Alliance. We bring best practices and successes to the table several times each year and on monthly calls. Often, private joint ventures and long-term business relationships are forged. In addition, members have access to other top marketing and sales experts, engaging in one-on-one conversations and cutting-edge strategies. Membership is by application only.

Individual Projects

In our experience, most small business owners and entrepreneurs who embrace the do-it-yourself approach are primarily tactically-focused. When they do seek outside copywriters or other professionals it is usually to create specific individual campaigns and projects. We offer project-based marketing services, but our primary purpose is to provide specific project help for our done-with-you clients. Having your marketing projects done one-by-one is by far the most expensive approach, although the initial amount may be — or certainly *appear* to be — less.

The biggest disadvantage in this approach is that by creating your marketing on a per-project basis, each project is effectively created and performed in a vacuum, with little connection into your overall Strategy. We are often contacted by or referred to prospects who have had many different campaigns and approaches mixed together over a period of time, some good and some not-so-good, with no consistency or congruence among them. The only time we recommend relying on the piecemeal Individual Project approach is when a clearly-planned program has fallen short or a fixed deadline is looming.

Referral Partners

When you have a good Strategic Plan in place, your offerings and Message are on-point and your Marketing and Sales are working well together, you may still have need assistance in specific areas. Having a Referral Partner you can call on, who understands your business enough to match you with other providers or Joint Ventures can be the difference between good and *great* success.

Sometimes it's just knowing the right program or software. In most cases, compensation is either paid by the Referral Partner or through an affiliate relationship. If you have specific needs, we have hundreds of providers and JV partners in our database to help. You can find some of our resources on our website at **www.Why2Wealth.com**.

Free Options

When it comes to investing in your business success, one of our mentors used to joke that, of all the choices out there, the "school of hard knocks" was the most expensive and time-consuming. While there are many free reports, eBooks, webinars, whitepapers, etc., there really is no "free" option to grow your business. Every path chosen involves some level of investment of ***Time, Money or Change.*** The faster and greater the return on your investment, the more change and financial commitment upfront. Of the three, the easiest to measure is money. Change is the hardest challenge to overcome and time is probably the most expensive.

However, we've mentioned a couple of free resources throughout this book — here are the links again:

Why-To-Wealth Blueprint™
www.MoreThanStrategy.com

Why-To-Wealth Action Questions™
www.Why2Wealth.com

If you haven't already done so, be sure to download these to help you on your journey. And we encourage you to make the decision now to implement the change necessary to allow your business to grow to its full potential, to provide the life and lifestyle you deserve. As a closing thought, consider this insight from John F. Kennedy…

> "There are risks and costs to a program of action — but they are far less than the long-range costs of comfortable inaction."

Carpe diem!

EMERSON BRANTLEY
TIMOTHY R. JOHNSON

For any other inquiries on how you can implement the concepts in this book, or have Emerson Brantley or Tim Johnson work with your business to take it to a higher, more productive and profitable level, contact us at Why-To-Wealth directly at:

Emerson@Why2Wealth.com
+1 904.419.7342

or

Tim@Why2Wealth.com
+1 904.242.6738

Thank you for investing in

S.O.L.D.

The Breakthrough System to Sell Less and Make More

Please visit the following websites for these bonus resources that will assist with the implementation of the concepts in this book:

Why-To-Wealth Blueprint™
www.MoreThanStrategy.com

Why-To-Wealth Action Questions™
www.Why2Wealth.com